The Open Text: New Directions for Biblical Studies?

The Open Text:

New Directions for Biblical Studies?

edited by
Francis Watson

SCM PRESS LTD

ISBN 0 334 02227 4

First published 1993
by SCM Press Ltd
26–30 Tottenham Road, London N1 4BZ

Typeset by Regent Typesetting, London
and printed in Great Britain by
Mackays of Chatham, Kent

'… lest we should be burdened with a closed book and so remain unfed.'

Martin Luther

Contents

Preface

All but one of the papers in this collection originated in a conference on 'New Directions for Biblical Studies?', organized by Leslie Houlden and myself and held at King's College London, 30 March–2 April 1992. We are grateful not only to the main speakers but also to the 130 or so participants who ensured a lively and fruitful discussion, and whose presence at the conference confirmed both that genuinely 'new directions' are wanted and that they seem increasingly possible. We would also like to express our gratitude to Mrs Claire Waddell for bearing the brunt of the administrative work so efficiently, calmly and cheerfully.

Francis Watson

King's College London
26 October 1992

Introduction: The Open Text

Francis Watson

The student who undertakes a conventional academic course in biblical studies will not only encounter a number of interesting perspectives on ancient Israel and the early church but will also be invited to join a community. Every academic discipline must transfer to the next generation an arcane body of knowledge – a heterogeneous collection of perspectives, information, practices and evaluations of which outsiders are largely ignorant – in order to initiate new recruits into the community, thus ensuring its future survival. In the case of biblical studies, however, the communal aspect of the discipline is given a unique (and uniquely problematic) shape by its relationship to a much larger and more significant community, the Christian church. On the one hand, the academic study of the Bible often occurs within church-based institutional structures and is an essential requirement for those entering most branches of the Christian ministry. On the other hand, its primary location within the secular university causes it to assert its independence from the church matrix and thus its equal standing with other academic disciplines. The result is an ambivalent relationship between the two communities, the academic and the ecclesial, expressed in the tendency to regard the church's understanding of scripture as that which the academic community must liberate us from.

On this view, the church traditionally understands scripture as an authoritative witness to its own dogmas, whereas the tradition of historical-critical scholarship frees the biblical texts from the control of these later dogmas by pointing to the fundamental significance of the historical contexts in which they originated. Even within institutional contexts oriented towards the church, initiation into this body of knowledge entails an awareness of what is taken to be an unbridgeable gulf between 'traditional beliefs' and 'modern knowledge'. Initiation into this academic community therefore requires the internalizing of *a story of salvation* with obvious roots in the Enlightenment's critique of 'positive' religion, and, behind that, in the Reformation's critique of post-biblical innovations within the church. Once, in pre-critical times (and in many places 'pre-critical times' still persist), the meaning and significance of the biblical texts was concealed by the doctrinal structures erected on top of them. But now, with the coming of the historical-critical gospel, their true meaning and significance can (in principle, if not always in practice) at last be laid bare. We have passed from darkness into light.

The essays in this collection do not attempt to put this story into reverse; they do not deny the possibility, necessity and enduring significance of historical-critical practice; but they do spring from a widespread sense that the story of salvation that has shaped its self-understanding is no longer credible in its traditional form. It is no longer plausible to identify the products of historical-critical discovery and hypothesis with the full reality of the biblical texts. Where historical questions are put to the texts, the texts will no doubt return the appropriate historical answers, but this circular process offers no guarantee that the initial questions constitute the only legitimate means of access to them. If the biblical texts can be construed as 'historical documents', they can just as well be construed as literary works or as resources for contemporary theological construction. In any case, what does it mean for a text to be a 'historical document'? Does it necessarily mean that the communal contexts in which these texts have historically functioned must be bypassed as of no consequence for the interpretative task?

This new, pluralist theoretical perspective now seems blindingly obvious to a significant minority of biblical scholars, even if its practical consequences have yet to be fully worked out. It is inadequate to see this situation as a retreat from the rigours of historical investigation back to the comforts of a neo-conservative view of the Bible.[1] While retreat rather than advance is always a possibility, the factors that have produced the current hermeneutical revolution will not be removed merely by appeals to the true path of conventional historical research. I shall point to four such factors.

2

Introduction

1. The postmodern condition

In an influential formulation, Jean-François Lyotard has defined our 'postmodern condition' as 'incredulity toward metanarratives.'[2] Theories offering a comprehensive account of significant reality prove unable to maintain their totalitarian claim in the face of the irreducible heterogeneity of reality as currently experienced. Shorn of much of their purported explanatory power, they are to be understood as stories told within determinate communal contexts alongside other communally-located stories. The Enlightenment's claim that humankind can be liberated from the darkness of superstition and tyranny by the light of reason is a prime example of a metanarrative of this kind, and the conventional self-understanding of biblical studies is in turn an excellent example of this metanarrative in concrete application. Yet the theme of 'the Bible in the modern world', in which the ancient text is made to conform to a monolithic 'modern world' or 'modern thought', now seems embarrassingly dated as a legitimation of the presence of biblical studies within the university. The Bible in a *post*modern world – the dawning perspective on the Bible within which the studies in this book seek to operate – would be a more surprising, demanding and interesting book than its rather bland modernist predecessor.

2. Opening the closed book

The genre of the biblical writings as the canonical texts of the Christian community has always generated expectations in their readers which sober, scholarly, literal-minded exegesis is unwilling and unable to meet.[3] It is this expectation that Luther defends, writing as a late mediaeval exponent of a pluralistic hermeneutic and not yet as a reformer, when in a preface to his early lectures on the psalms he expresses his concern 'lest we should be burdened with a closed book and so remain unfed' (*ne clauso libro oneremur et non vescamur*).[4] This statement, which provides the superscription for the present collection, offers us the image of the 'closed book' against which may be set the counter-image of 'the open text'. The closed book is the biblical text as enclosed in an academic institution which licenses a single, restricted interpretative paradigm within which one must operate if one wishes to enjoy the rewards that are on offer. The open text is the biblical text as the site of a proliferation of meanings that accords with its character as a sacred text, constantly read and reread without ever being exhausted. The pluralist, postmodern moment in contemporary biblical studies might therefore be seen as the rediscovery of this old, suppressed possibility.

3. *The literary paradigm*

Surveys of the history of modern biblical interpretation typically portray a linear development in which, for example, source criticism, form criticism and redaction criticism follow one another in orderly succession, each arising at its appointed moment as if by providential design. Despite the tensions between such enterprises as these, the claim that there are elements of continuity as well as discontinuity here remains plausible, for all are held together by a general orientation towards diachronic historical reconstruction. However, the past two decades have seen the development of a 'synchronic' approach, influenced by structuralism, new criticism and other trends in literary studies, which has been successfully applied especially to biblical narrative. While it is possible to argue that narrative criticism of the gospels represents a 'natural' or 'logical' development beyond redaction criticism, the new form of interpretation can be practised in relative independence from the old: its characteristic insights derive precisely from *ignoring* the findings of source, form and redaction criticism.[5] Biblical scholars are concerned primarily with the practice of exegesis, and the development of a successful alternative to conventional exegesis is a sign that the acknowledgment of pluralism at the theoretical level has important consequences on the level of practice.[6]

4. *From author to reader*

Modern hermeneutics and literary theory have introduced a major redefinition of the task of interpretation, shifting the focus of interest from the intention of the author to the active participation of the reader in producing the meaning of the text. Biblical studies has traditionally emphasized the importance of authorial intention, regarded as a guarantee of the text's relative coherence and meaningfulness; the role of the interpreter was simply to bring to light that partially hidden coherence and meaningfulness, by reconstructing the original context as fully as possible. In this approach, the interpreter was cast in a role which was supposed to be 'objective' and 'neutral', uncommitted to any value except the service of the truth, however unpopular that truth might prove. Recognition of the impossibility of this self-definition has come from many quarters. Feminist analysis has shown that the results of allegedly objective and neutral investigation are often marked by the androcentric bias of male interpreters. Political analysis has questioned whether the needs of the contemporary world are best served by an interpretative practice which in many respects seeks to disengage itself from that world. Deconstruction challenges all claims to textual coherence or unified meaning, bringing to light the repressions upon which they are founded. There has been a marked revival of interest in the history of a text's interpretation, in belated recognition of the difficulty of distinguishing the meaning of the text from what is has been taken to mean by its readers.[7]

These factors in the current situation are of course open to very diverse assessment and do not amount to a unified programme. It remains possible and plausible to argue that historical research, in continuity with its previous development, will continue to play a major role in the biblical interpretation of the future, and that challenges to its previous self-understanding have not succeeded in discrediting the entire enterprise.[8] It is also possible and plausible to claim that the new interpretative possibilities are finite, that they only become possible because of the constraints that limit and define them, and that they can only establish themselves in constant dialogue with existing possibilities; success or failure will be dependent on the persuasiveness with which they do so. The situation, though fluid, is certainly not the wild libertarian paradise desired by some and feared by others. Structures are changing, but they are still structures.[9]

This cautionary note is sounded in Mark Brett's essay in this volume, which points to the need for critical assessment of the claims made by or on behalf of various forms of 'reader criticism'. The most radical claim – that readers bear *sole* responsibility for the production of meaning – turns out to make no difference at all to the practice of interpretation. Brett carefully and clearly analyses some of the different ways in which the figure of 'the reader' is employed in contemporary interpretation and theory, and discovers a number of points of convergence with conventional historical-critical practice.

Biblical studies has nothing to fear from a pluralistic situation in which different types of interpretation derive from the varying interests of interpreters.

The title of Phyllis Trible's essay – 'Treasures Old and New: Biblical Theology and the Challenge of Feminism' – also acknowledges that the previous history of the discipline should not simply be discarded. Yet the maleness of the authors of major Old Testament theologies (Eichrodt, von Rad and so on) proves to be not an irrelevance but a significant factor in the inadequacy of their proposals. Trible points to a number of areas where recent feminist study of the Bible has succeeded in exposing the limitations of patriarchal scholarship. Her acknowledgment that not all feminist perspectives agree or will endure points to a capacity for *self*-criticism which unsympathetic outsiders often fail to notice in feminist analysis. But the main intent is constructive: to disclose points in the biblical texts which offer the promise of a new biblical theology responsive to feminist concerns.

Like Trible's, my own contribution attempts to combine hermeneutical reflection, exegetical practice, and an overarching theological concern. Taking the 'parable of the sheep and the goats' (Matt. 25.31–46) as a test-case, I try to show that the integration of the concerns of liberation theology into First World biblical exegesis is facilitated by openness to the new hermeneutical perspectives, while it remains extremely difficult within the constraints of the historical-critical method. Over against the common assumption that theological reflection should occur (if at all) only *after* a firm exegetical foundation has been laid, I wish to explore the possibility of an exegesis directed from the outset by theological questions.

Werner Jeanrond is primarily a systematic theologian rather than a biblical scholar, and he too expresses the view that the current hermeneutical revolution suggests new approaches to the old problem of the gulf between biblical studies and Christian theology. Jeanrond opposes the imposition of pre-existing theological positions on to the biblical texts as vigorously as any biblical scholar, but he also believes that biblical studies loses its legitimacy when it insists upon a rigidly historical, non-theological agenda. It must learn to regard itself as a pluralistic discipline in which the theological perspective has its proper place; and this theological perspective would itself have to be pluralistic, in keeping with the many-faceted biblical texts. According to Jeanrond, 'it simply does not make sense that theologians today are not actively engaged in studying the primary texts of their traditions, while their biblical colleagues are on the whole not involved in discussing the intellectual, cultural, political, social and ecclesial context in which the textual objects of their study could play a transformative role.'

One of the exclusions upon which the historical-critical paradigm is based is the proscription of the tradition of allegorical interpretation derived from Philo and the patristic period. Allegory has been regarded as sheer wilfulness and arbitrariness, the antithesis of what responsible biblical interpretation ought to be. Frances Young argues that the hermeneutical revolution enables and necessitates the reopening of this issue. Allegory can be more sympathetically seen as the activity of making connections between one text and another and between the text and life, within the broad context of the entire biblical story. A discussion of the various functions of allegorical interpretation during the patristic period is linked with the contemporary rediscovery of the role of the reader. The historical-critical tradition has resulted in a theological impoverishment which the older interpretative tradition can help us to remedy.

Stephen Moore reflects on modern interpretation of the New Testament's representation of the death of Christ in the light of a central text of poststructuralist theory and historiography, Michel Foucault's *Discipline and Punish*. Foucault analyses the enlightened humanitarianism that, from the eighteenth century onwards, criticizes the notion of punishment as stemming from the all-powerful, vindictive will of an absolute monarch who embodies the law. According to Foucault, the development of disciplinary practices designed to facilitate the subject's *self*-disciplining and self-regulation serves merely to extend the power of the disciplinary institution. Moore draws an illuminating parallel with the displacement of a penal substitutionary view of the atonement by a subjective view oriented towards the transformation of the self. In so doing, he further illustrates the fruitfulness for biblical scholarship of a close engagement with current literary theory. Biblical scholars must broaden the range of their reading.

Sociological analysis of the biblical texts occupies an ambivalent position in the field of 'new directions for biblical studies'. On the one hand, it clearly *is* a 'new direction', deriving not only from the prior history of the discipline but also from interdisciplinary links. On the other hand, it typically serves to reinforce the perception that interpretation must be concerned exclusively with historical realities from which the interpreter remains disengaged. Stephen Barton presents a critique of the recent use of the sociological category of the 'sect' in New Testament studies, revealing the ways in which interpreters who impose this modern category remain locked within the hermeneutical circle they try to escape. Sociological approaches to biblical texts are to be distinguished from 'literary' or 'canonical' ones not by virtue of their superior objectivity but in terms of the different aims that interpreters may legitimately adopt. Barton thus illustrates the importance of hermeneutical awareness in the evaluation of *historical* research: there can be no clear line of demarcation between hermeneutically- and historically-oriented scholarship.

To advocate feminist or liberationist perspectives, interpretative pluralism, poststructuralist theory and the like is, inevitably, to define oneself as belonging to an avant-garde within current biblical studies – a position which of course gives no guarantees as to the quality or relevance of one's work. Such a position tends to generate the optical illusion that the old ways are moribund and that a successful revolution is only just over the horizon. But this is to overlook the fact that the old ways continue to show surprising vitality, and that the new ones do not always achieve the rapid acceptance they believe they deserve. As Richard Coggins points out, the genre of the commentary represents a kind of bastion of critical orthodoxy, and commentaries continue to be produced in very large numbers. There are increasing signs that radical hermeneutical questions are making an impact here too. But old issues refuse to lie down and die: the relation between scholarly and devotional requirements, the question of objectivity, the primacy of historical exegesis – such matters are still with us, especially in exegetical practice.

Forsaking editorial discretion and adopting the role of a critical reader, I shall in conclusion offer some reflections on areas in which contributions to this volume seem to me to diverge or dissent, or in which clarifications are needed. I hope that other readers will also sense the many common threads tying our various essays together. But, since we are in different ways all advocating a pluralist hermeneutic, and since a pluralism without dissent would issue only in a breakdown of communication, differences must also be acknowledged.

Introduction

1. Pluralism as end or as means

To advocate pluralism within biblical studies is to resist the assumption that only historical approaches to the texts are acceptable. But why should one want to resist this assumption? Is it because pluralism, the convergence of as many different approaches to the text as possible, is inherently a good thing? This would mean that, so long as a particular mode of interpretation contributed another perspective to the plurality, its specific perspective or direction would be immune from criticism. Yet it might prove important to discuss why and to what purpose one engages in biblical interpretation in the first place. If one such purpose seemed much more important than another, would it be appropriate to criticize the resulting interpretative practice on the grounds that it failed to promote plurality?

2. Hermeneutics and theology

All contributions to this book avail themselves of insights that have recently entered the discipline from philosophical hermeneutics and from literary theory. Hermeneutics – using the term in a broad sense – is, in the humanities, becoming a discipline in its own right, and biblical scholars are beginning to offer their own contribution to it. Although there is nothing inherently theological about this emergent interdisciplinary discipline, it has been welcomed by some as a bridge between biblical studies and theology. Others, however, show no particular inclination to locate their hermeneutical interests within an overarching theological project. The question is therefore whether hermeneutics simply offers us important but general perspectives on textual interpretation, or whether it also provides new resources for addressing a specifically theological problem.

3. What is 'theology'?

Among those who announce their concern for 'theology', there is a lack of agreement or clarity about just what this object is supposed to be. Is an interpretative practice 'theological' if it arises from the interpreter's personal engagement (existential or political) with the biblical text? Should a theologically-oriented mode of interpretation issue in 'realist' assertions about God and the world, or can it confine itself within the bounds of textuality? Are we speaking primarily of 'Christian' theology, or are we at least as interested in post-Christian or non-Christian forms? In seeking to bridge the gulf between biblical studies and theology, is one also seeking to bridge the gulf between the academy and the Christian community?

4. Trust and suspicion

A distinction has emerged in hermeneutical discussion between a 'hermeneutic of trust' and a 'hermeneutic of suspicion' (the terminology varies).[10] Most would agree that our attitude towards the texts we study should be neither wholly positive (a determination to affirm them no matter what) nor wholly negative (a refusal to say anything good about them); no one wishes to appear either gullible or misanthropic. Yet it proves difficult for the interpreter to be both trusting and suspicious at one and the same time. Is the interpreter's fundamental motivation the belief that the biblical texts, seen in a certain light, have something important to offer us in our contemporary impoverishment? Or is the fundamental motivation the belief that these texts have been and are still detrimental to human well-being, a situation which their status as sacred objects makes it all the more important to expose? Alternatively, is it possible to construe the relation of interpreter to text in a way that escapes this antithesis of trust and suspicion?

5. The question of ideology

The term 'ideological' is occasionally employed in these essays in very different senses.[11] On the one hand, it can be used to designate 'committed' or 'engaged' modes of interpretation in which the interpreter is pursuing certain socio-political goals. A negative evaluation enters this initially neutral term when the commitment is pursued in a manner which is held to be too exclusive or too uncritical. On the other hand, the term 'ideological' is also used by 'committed' interpreters in something like its classical Marxist sense: as designating a discourse one of whose functions is the concealment of oppressive social relations. The former usage accords with the postmodern view of pluralism as an end in itself; an interpretation becomes 'ideological' in a pejorative sense when it raises itself above the plurality and claims some form of normative status for itself. The latter usage implies the kind of truth-claim that cannot be entirely at home in the sceptical, relativizing climate of postmodernity. Underlying this difference of usage is an ambivalence or a disagreement about the scope for a political dimension within exegetical, hermeneutical and theological discourse.

But it is time to allow the contributors to speak for themselves.

Notes

1. This is, with some qualifications, the view of John Barton in *People of the Book? The Authority of the Bible in Christianity*, London: SPCK 1988.
2. J.-F. Lyotard, *The Postmodern Condition: A Report on Knowledge*, Manchester: Manchester University Press 1984, xxiv.
3. Werner Jeanround points out that 'genre' is determined not only by the text but also by its reception (*Text and Interpretation as Categories of Theological Thinking* [ET Dublin: Gill and Macmillan 1988], 105). It therefore cannot be claimed that the canonizing of the biblical texts represents a 'mistake' about their genre.
4. *WA* 55/1.10.14–15.
5. Phyllis Trible's literary-feminist readings of texts from the Hebrew Bible also illustrate the independence of such an approach from conventional diachronic concerns; see her *God and the Rhetoric of Sexuality*, Philadelphia: Fortress Press 1978; London: SCM Press 1992, and *Texts of Terror: Literary-Feminist Readings of Biblical Narratives* Philadelphia: Fortress Press 1984; London: SCM Press 1992.
6. For a survey and assessment of this development, see Stephen D. Moore, *Literary Criticism and the Gospels: The Theoretical Challenge*, New Haven and London: Yale University Press 1989.
7. Frances Young employs the analogy of the musical performance to point to the difficulty and unhelpfulness of this distinction, in *The Art of Performance: Towards a Theology of Holy Scripture*, London: Darton, Longman & Todd 1990. The text (musical or biblical) is nothing without repeated, differing actualizations in performance. In general, we do not need to know where, say, Beethoven's intentions end and those of the contemporary performer take over; what matters is whether the performance is effective or not, a judgment for which musical tradition offers reasonably clear criteria. (The situation recalls the well-known closing line of W.B. Yeats' poem, 'Among School Children': 'How can we know the dancer from the dance?')

8. Compare Mark G. Brett, *Biblical Criticism in Crisis? The impact of the canonical approach on Old Testament studies*, Cambridge: Cambridge University Press 1991, 11–13.

9. While Stephen Moore's *Mark and Luke in Poststructuralist Perspectives. Jesus Begins to Write* (New Haven and London: Yale University Press 1992) goes much further in a libertarian direction than most biblical scholars would be willing or able to follow, it is nevertheless steeped in existing (poststructuralist) textual practices.

10. Stephen C. Barton alludes to this distinction when he argues that the gospels' status as scripture makes them 'the basis for a *trustful* exegesis in which theologically-informed faith, reason, experience and imagination enable their fruitful interpretation and appropriation in the Church today' ('Women, Jesus and the Gospels', in *Who Needs Feminism?*, ed. Richard Holloway, London: SPCK 1991, 32–58; 34–35 [my italics]. For a more 'suspicious' hermeneutic, see my 'Strategies of Recovery and Resistance: Hermeneutical Reflections on Genesis 1–3 and its Pauline Reception', *Journal for the Study of the New Testament* 45 (1992), 79–103.

11. On this terminological and substantive problem see Terry Eagleton, *Ideology: An Introduction*, London and New York: Verso 1991, 1–31; Robert P. Carroll, 'Ideology', in *A Dictionary of Biblical Interpretation*, ed. R.J. Coggins and J.L. Houlden, London: SCM Press and Philadelphia: Trinity Press International 1990, 309–11.

1

The Future of Reader Criticisms?

Mark G. Brett

Our recent debates about method in biblical studies might appear to be merely a local skirmish within the guild of biblical scholarship. But the issues are not merely local. Indeed, biblical studies is just one theatre in a much bigger methodological war taking place throughout the humanities. Perhaps the most fierce battles have taken place in North America under the broad heading of 'literary theory', but the wider implications of this war have touched many disciplines both inside and outside North America.

The rise of literary theory has been associated with a new and unsettling attention to factors which influence the process of interpretation, factors like gender, race, culture and class. The possibility of objectivity has been widely questioned, and changes to the curriculum have been greeted in many quarters with dismay and alarm. The various post-structuralist schools, for example, have even been accused of undermining the very social fabric of Western societies.[1] Literary theory is for some not just an irritation to the real business of scholarship; it is a social menace.

The disposition of this paper is not so apocalyptic. Let us entertain the hypothesis that not all literary theories are demons in disguise; let us begin with the charitable expectation that they may well have some important points to make, as long as one is patient enough to learn a new vocabulary. On the other hand, one also needs to be charitable to the scholars of the past; they should not be treated as simply grist to the mill of hermeneutical Enlightenment. I have recently suggested that the concept of authorial intention, for example, is still perfectly respectable as long as one has a rigorous enough understanding of intentionality. The advent of reader theory does not necessarily imply the death of authors. I have not argued that one should always and everywhere seek to discover the author's intention. On the contrary, the question of what an author might have intended to communicate to his or her original audience is only one of several questions critics might bring to a text. Reader criticisms bring another set of questions. My position is pluralist: there are a wide range of questions one might bring to a text, and therefore it is appropriate to have a wide range of methods in order to answer those questions. To put it another way, there are several different kinds of interpretative interest, and properly conceived, they need not cancel each other out. For example, there are different kinds of intentions and there are different kinds of readers;[2] one method may be intentionalist and another readerly, but they may not be in direct competition.

Notice the all-important qualification: interpretative interests need to be *properly conceived*. I suspect that some of the talk about reader criticism has been conceptually confused. In this paper, I will not attempt to provide a comprehensive survey of reader criticisms and their applications in biblical studies; rather, the focus will be on three issues that have proved conceptually problematic and which are relevant to any future development of reader criticisms: first, the relationship between epistemology and the goals of reader criticism; second, the relationship between reader criticisms and historical questions; and third, the relationship between the ethical or ideological commitments of readers and the critical method that they choose to adopt.

Epistemology and the Goals of Reader Criticism

Reader critics are sometimes tempted to think that their own approach has rectified a fatal methodological flaw in previous studies. This then leads to an anti-pluralist argument which runs something like this: over the past three decades fashions have simply changed in hermeneutics. We used to be interested in authorial intention, then we were interested in texts as such, and now we are interested in readers.[3] The trouble with the emphasis on authors, so this story goes, was that it hadn't discovered the so-called intentional fallacy, and therefore failed to notice that texts have a kind of public existence independent of their authors. The trouble with the emphasis on texts in themselves was that it attributed too much independence and coherence to literary artifacts and failed to realize that meaning is always created by readers. Thus, reader criticism arises from the ashes of both intentionalism and formalism.

As an example of this progressivist attitude to hermeneutical theory, let us consider the ground-breaking work of Edgar Conrad, recently published in the Overtures to Biblical Theology series. This book, *Reading Isaiah*, presents a fresh and illuminating interpretation of the whole of Isaiah, and as a work of exegesis it deserves serious attention. But the methodological preface to this work should be treated with more circumspection. Conrad rightly says that he needed to suspend all the previous theories about the development of the book, its various authors and editors, in order to focus afresh on his experience of reading the text as a whole. After all, we have no independent evidence for the development of the book; all we have is the text of Isaiah itself. Conrad then suggests that what was primary in his method was the interaction between text and reader. So far so good. But then he invokes a theoretical argument which is meant to lend some authority to his method. He supplies a lengthy quotation from Stanley Fish's book, *Is There a Text in this Class?*, which demonstrates the unavoidablity of the reader's contribution to textual meaning. The inevitable conclusion, we are told, is that all talk of authorial intention as an interpretative goal needs to be given up as illusory; intention is a deeply problematic concept that apparently only belongs to the unenlightened days of historical criticism.

But this is not what Fish actually says. His point is not so much about interpretative goals as about epistemology. Let me quote from the passage chosen by Conrad:

> Rather than intention and its formal realization producing interpretation (the 'normal' picture), interpretation *creates* intention and its formal realization by creating the conditions in which it becomes possible to pick them out.[4]

The main point is that authorial intention is always the product of critical reconstruction. We cannot know an author's mind directly; it is not a bit of evidence independent of the process of interpretation. This epistemological point does not so much prohibit an interest in authorial intention as encourage an appropriate sense of scholarly humility. It is not so much the goals of exegesis which need to change but our attitude to how these goals might be achieved. According to

Fish, all scholarship is the product of interpretative communities; all interpretation is socially constructed. We are dealing here with general philosophical reflections on the nature of reading, no matter what method we adopt, no matter what school of criticism. *All* interpretation is said to be the product of reader construction, and if you could find a method that wasn't, then Fish's main argument would fall to the ground.

Indeed, in his later book, *Doing What Comes Naturally*, Fish even suggests that we cannot do *without* some notion of authorial intention. For example, in response to the legal theorist Ronald Dworkin who argues for the disposal of authorial intention, Fish replies quite clearly to the contrary: 'One cannot understand an utterance without at *the same time* hearing or reading it as the utterance of someone with more or less specific concerns, ... someone with an intention.' In other words, this lover of paradox wants to assure us that the presumption of intentionality is unavoidable. Fish is not going back on his previous position; he does not mean to imply that intention is something outside a text which can guide or constrain interpretation. On the contrary, intention is itself seen as the product of interpretation; he repeats his view that 'Intentions are not self-declaring, but must be constructed from evidence that is itself controversial'.[5] Still less is he supporting avowed intentionalists in their attempt to claim the moral high ground. But he does want to say that, unlike Dworkin, he has no methodological prescriptions or recommendations at all; he is simply asserting an epistemological necessity.[6]

To summarize my argument to this point: some biblical critics have invoked Fish's work as a means of legitimating methodological changes in biblical studies.[7] Although it is true to say that Fish is perhaps the most famous and elegant reader theorist, it would be mistaken to think that his views actually make any methodological difference. At most, the notion of interpretative communities offers an explanation of the deep conflicts in biblical studies; it does not represent a change in method or a change in interpretative goals. Even if Fish succeeds in making us think that all interpretations are merely the contruction of a reader, or school of readers, then he has only persuaded us to adopt a general philosophical position. He wants to say that *all* interpretation is implicitly reader criticism. It follows that any concern with sources, form and redaction and authors are *also* readerly concerns. Since Fish does not wish to distinguish reader criticism from any other kind of criticism,[8] it is still possible to adopt his philosophy of interpretation and, at the same time, to be interested in authorial intentions and other old-fashioned concepts.

So the question arises, then: is there a distinctive method or strategy of reader criticism? In this context, we shall consider two distinctive methods. The first, chronological reading, is essentially indifferent to historical questions, and the second, reception theory, is in many respects barely distinguishable from the historical criticism that has been practised in biblical studies for the last century or so.

Chronological Reading: A Distinctive Method

One early essay by Fish really does make a methodological difference, and that is the first one in *Is There a Text in this Class?*, 'Literature in the Reader: Affective Stylistics'. One needs to note immediately, however, that this essay was only reprinted as a monument to an earlier Fish who had been superseded by all the other essays. This earlier Fish was reflecting on his study of Milton, *Surprised by Sin* (1967) which undermined the prevailing methods of criticism at the time. Fish argued that the basic error in both New Criticism and Structuralism was that they can only provide an interpretation *after* the entire text has been read. The experience of reading Milton, however, suggested that what was really important was not the retrospective view of the whole text, but rather the developing responses of readers as they worked their way through the text.

This method Fish called 'affective stylistics', partly in response to a view of stylistics which Michael Riffaterre had developed independently of Fish. Subsequently, Wolfgang Iser developed a similar strategy of reading, and it was especially Iser's work which became influential in Gospel studies. Despite their differences, the earlier works of Fish, Riffaterre and Iser represent a distinct strategy for interpretation which emphasizes the twists and turns of the text as they are experienced in chronological order. This style of reading has been variously called chronological, temporal or sequential. These terms refer not to a reconstructed historical sequence but to the temporal sequence of reading a text. Gaps, ambiguities, and questions are not to be prematurely resolved; they are actually constitutive of the reading experience at particular points in the poem or narrative. To take a brief biblical example, in Gen. 32.24 the narrator tells us that Jacob was alone at the river Jabbok and that a man wrestled with him until daybreak. The assailant is simply called 'a man', and that ambiguity is a constituent feature of the narrative at that point. Only later do we have Jacob's realization that this man was actually God.

A more extended example can be found in Robert Fowler's first book on Mark's Gospel, *Loaves and Fishes* (1981). Several scholars had noted the verbal similarities between Mark 14.22 in the narrative of the last supper and Mark 6.41 in the feeding of the five thousand. There is a clear connection between the two narratives, but how is this connection to be construed? Fowler argues for a chronological reading in which the sequence of the stories is observed; the fuller significance of the feeding story is not yet known and should not be prematurely introduced; there are no eucharistic overtones at this stage. Only retrospectively does the ideal reader perceive the connection. But the feeding story in Mark 6 also sets up an expectation on the reader's part which is relevant to the feeding of the four thousand in chapter 8. In ch. 8 the disciples respond to a very similar situation by saying: 'How can one feed these people with bread here in the desert?' The Gospel writer, according to Fowler, has inserted the feeding of the five thousand prior to the more traditional story of ch. 8 in order to heighten the reader's amazement at the obtuseness of the disciples. Thus, a chronological reading explores the unfolding of the narrative, as the reader's anticipations and recollections twist and turn through the nuances of character and allusion.[9]

Fowler's work can be considered a good example of the chronological strategy of reading, but we should notice that the theoretical inspirations for *Loaves and Fishes* come not from one source but from a blend of sequential reading with redaction criticism and narrative criticism. One could question whether this is a logically consistent blend of approaches. Fowler continues to make claims about the history of the material and the intentions of a redactor while, at the same time, emphasizing that the reader should operate only with knowledge *intrinsic to the text*. This reader is opposed to one with extrinsic knowledge, say, of eucharistic traditions in the early church. Fowler suggests that 'far greater authority must be accorded the text itself to inform, control and mould its reader'. This approach, he insists, 'restores to the text its rightful measure of autonomy'.[10] But the idea that literary texts are autonomous is precisely the New Critical idea that reader theories sought to undermine. Thus, we need to conclude that when Fowler uses the sequential strategy of reading he is still, in fact, operating with some key assumptions of New Criticism.

But the more important point to make is that even if Fowler was thoroughly consistent in his application of reader criticism, the strategy of sequential reading would nevertheless be heavily indebted to formalism, i.e., to a mode of reading which was relatively indifferent to the historical background of a text. Iser, for example, emphasizes that texts are not autonomous entities; they leave gaps which need to be filled out by interpretation. Exegesis is therefore an *interaction between* text and reader. But there are two senses in which Iser's work may be considered only a moderate revision of New Criticism. First, he sees only a limited range of possible readings which are finally constrained by the text itself. Second, he is careful to distinguish between his own theory of reader-response which has its 'roots in the text' and a theory of reception which investigates the successive readings of actual historical audiences.[11] The theory of reception is associated more with Iser's colleague at the University of Constance, Hans-Robert Jauss. Iser's implicit reader (like Wayne Booth's 'implied' reader) is a trans-historical ideal who works with information supplied by the text and only by the text; Jauss, on the other hand, seeks to reconstruct the expectations and changing receptions of actual historical audiences. Iser and Jauss have produced not one but two entirely different versions of reader theory and they themselves sum up the difference in a distinction between the 'implicit' reader and the 'historical' reader.[12] Fowler's version of reader-response is situated much closer to Iser, and together they represent a group of critics who have only slightly diverged from New Critical theories of textual autonomy. In this formalist group, we should include Willem Vorster's work on the Succession Narrative and David Clines's recent work on Genesis.[13]

We should not, however, seek to dismiss Iser's divergence from New Criticism as being of no consequence at all. Stanley Fish, for example, repudiates his own early strategy of chronological reading by claiming that it was merely 'a turn of the new critical screw'.[14] Subsequently, he launched a full-scale attack on Iser's residual formalism in a paper entitled 'Who's Afraid of Wolfgang Iser?'.

However, as we have seen, the later Fish does not in fact deliver anything that might claim to be a distinctive strategy of reading.[15] Chronological reading can at least claim a measure of distinctiveness, and in this respect it has more practical consequences for biblical studies than the epistemology of the later Fish.

But the method of sequential reading is only one version among many reader criticisms, and the other versions represent more thorough reactions against New Criticism. In biblical studies, we have recently seen a new emphasis amongst some critics on indeterminacy of meaning, a deconstructionist concept that is fundamentally at odds with the New Critical idea that texts can constrain interpretation. For example, David Gunn has attacked Meir Sternberg for apparently arguing that sequential readings of biblical narrative present only temporary indeterminacies that resolve themselves later in the reading process. Gunn responds by listing the narratives about Abram, Jephthah, Saul, and Job, arguing that the endings of these texts are more complex and mysterious than their beginnings.[16] Gunn is thereby aligning himself with the deconstructionist emphasis on indeterminacy. Many critics, however, now regard deconstructive reading as itself a new twist of formalism. They argue that deconstruction is too textual and lacks any significant attention to the embedding of texts in historical ideologies and practices.[17] Thus, the most recent battles in literary theory have been between different versions of deconstruction and the so-called New Historicism. But for the moment, we shall turn our attention to Hans-Robert Jauss's method of reader criticism.

Reception Theory

Beginning in the late 1960s, Jauss provided a catalyst for a fresh movement in literary criticism. He drew partly on the hermeneutical philosophy of Hans-Georg Gadamer who put forward the influential thesis that all interpretation is conditioned by substrata of historical influences which act on readers whether they are aware of this or not. Gadamer's was primarily a descriptive philosophy, and although he could not resist the occasional prescriptive remark, he never set out to provide a distinctive method for literary criticism. Jauss, on the other hand, critically appropriated Gadamer's work in formulating an approach that moved beyond the polarized situation in literary criticism at the time. He argued for a focus on the reception of literature, rejecting both the New Critical neglect of history, and the version of Marxism which reduced literary works to their original historical context. This school of Marxists, Jauss insisted, needed to explain how literary works survived their original contexts, while the formalists, on the other hand, needed to provide an explanation of why particular literary works are received differently in different historical periods. Jauss suggested that this fresh attention to the reconstruction of audience reception need not fall back into the naivety of older historicisms as long as literary scholars retained a measure of self-awareness. At the same time, reception studies would recover a proper sense of the historicality of all literature, falling neither into historical determinism nor into a neglect of history altogether.

Although Jauss's own work has apparently had very little influence in biblical studies, it seems that there has been a growing interest in the reception of biblical literature in publications of the last decade. This has no doubt been due to several factors, including perhaps the influence of Gadamer. But whatever the causes, we have seen, for example, a growing dissatisfaction with the practice of regarding 'secondary' additions to biblical texts as being of no intrinsic interest. On the contrary, these additions provide valuable clues as to how earlier material was being read within the biblical period itself. One need only refer to the magisterial work of Michael Fishbane *Biblical Interpretation in Ancient Israel* (1985), and to the widespread acclaim that it received, to appreciate just how scholarly attitudes have changed over the last two decades or so. In a similar vein to Fishbane's work, John Barton's *Oracles of God* (1986)[18] focussed on the reception of ancient prophecy in the second temple period, stressing the differences between pre-exilic perceptions and prophecy and perceptions of prophetic texts which grew up after the exile. Among the most striking claims of this book was the idea that the original audiences of apocalypses would have seen no distinction between prophecy and apocalyptic literature. Barton thereby identified an important question about how we should understand notions of genre. If the original audience did not see a distinction between prophecy and apocalypse, then what kind of distinction is this? This is just one of the fresh set of questions that reception studies have generated.

It may be important to recognize, however, that reception theory does not always throw up new questions; sometimes it simply recasts old questions in new vocabulary. Thus, although it is commonplace to suggest that biblical scholars always lag behind developments in literary theory, it is often the case that similar kinds of conclusions have long been arrived at without the benefit of a fashionable theoretical vocabulary.[19] Consider for example Jauss's proposal that the first task in a history of reception is to reconstruct the 'horizon of expectation' of the original audience, that is, to reconstruct the set of expectations that the first audience would have brought to a work. According to Jauss, the particular text in question is to be read against the background of 'those works the author explicitly or implicitly presupposed his contemporary audience to know'.[20] Turning to a classic example in biblical studies, one could say that Wellhausen was concerned with just this kind of historical question when he argued that the eighth-century prophet Amos presented an innovation in Israelite religion; in particular, there was no pre-existing theology of covenant law upon which the prophet was dependent. Later scholars argued otherwise, but they were all concerned with the same issue, namely, how the text of Amos was to be construed against its original background. The most important differences between Wellhausen and his critics turned not so much on what was in the text of Amos as on how we should construe the relationship *between* Amos and the religious climate into which the prophet originally spoke.

More recently, John Barton's study *Amos's Oracles Against the Nations* (1980) addresses this question in great detail without ever referring to reader critics like Iser or Jauss. The structure of Amos 1–2, Barton concludes, is designed to culminate in the oracle against Israel in 2.6ff. The prophet begins by condemning the war crimes of surrounding nations, and having secured the audience's agreement, Amos then rounds on his unsuspecting audience by proclaiming judgment against Israel on account of social injustices committed within the community. The overall effect was designed 'to produce surprise and horror in the intended audience'.[21] For this prophetic technique to be successful, Barton suggests, Amos must have held a definite set of beliefs about his intended audience. In particular, the audience would have thought that Israel had a specially privileged position which indemnified her against divine judgment, and moreover, they would not have regarded internal social sins as at all comparable with the gravity of war crimes.[22]

Barton's monograph on Amos raises a number of important

questions about the relationship between formalist and historical versions of reader criticism. First, his argument presupposes a notion of sequential reading similar to that found in Wolfgang Iser's work and in the early Stanley Fish. If the sequence of oracles in Amos 1–2 was designed to produce surprise and horror in the audience, and to disrupt their fundamental expectations, then we must presume an original audience who had no inkling of the condemnation that awaited them. The audience would have to be drawn into the prophet's rhetoric step by step until the sequence of indictments, and the growing moral outrage, was at the last moment turned full force against them.

Barton's hypothesis is attractive, but consider once again the evidence for this view. The hypothesis cannot be based on a transcript of the prophet's original oral delivery. On the contrary, the evidence is derived from a canonical text, i.e., a text which has been read, re-read, and edited, probably over a period of several hundred years. In a formalist, sequential reading this would not be a problem, since the formalist does not have real readers in view at all. The formalist requires only implied and ideal readers who are sensitive to every nuance of the text as it is shaped by the rhetoric of the implied author.[23] The formalist modestly constructs a reader who can explore all the interpretative possibilities of a text without yet claiming to know anything about the details of actual historical readers.

But Barton's hypothesis is more daring than this; he wants to say something about the historical intentions that lie behind the text, and the historical shocks and surprises that lay in store for the real, original audience. We must surmise, however, that these shocks and surprises could only last so long. It is surely implausible to imagine a hapless audience with a peculiar propensity to fall for the same prophetic trick over and over again.[24] On the contrary, Barton needs to suppose that even though the text of Amos was read, re-read, and edited over hundreds of years, it nevertheless preserved the basic sequence of Amos's oracles first against foreign nations and then against Israel. I am not arguing that this is an impossible presumption to make, only that it requires a certain optimism about the processes of textual preservation in ancient Israel.

Stephen Moore has recently made a related point about the possible relationship between sequential reading and historical studies. Several scholars have observed that modern ideas of reading have been shaped by the culture of the printing press. In the ancient world, most reading was public reading, and this was no doubt especially the case with the biblical literature. Moore has pointed out the irony in the fact that sequential reading does actually present an affinity with the aural experience of listening to a text being read aloud. When considering the audiences of the biblical period, it would be more accurate to speak of aural response rather than reader response. And as Walter Ong has emphasized, spoken words are events which 'never present all at once but occur seriatim, syllable-after-syllable'.[25] Thus, ironically, the formalist concern with sequential reader-responses may have inadvertently made a contribution to historical studies of textual reception. We need to remember, however, that a coherent formalism does not need to legitimate itself by contributing to historical questions; these are separate interpretative interests which should not simply be conflated. And as the example of Amos 1–2 shows, we should not imagine that the reading of canonical texts provides an unproblematic window through which to view the original audiences of the biblical texts.

If, however, the responses of the original audiences of biblical texts have to be imaginatively reconstructed, the matter is somewhat clearer when we come to consider the responses of modern readers. At least modern readers are our contemporaries, and there are greater amounts of data available which provide us with a clearer view of the circumstances of interpretation. We may even be able to ask contemporaries to clarify their responses. The final section of this paper is devoted to this modern end of the problem, and especially to the issue of how a modern reader's values and commitments might influence interpretation.

Reader Commitments and Critical Methods

Reader criticism has sometimes been associated with such a strong emphasis on the plurarity of possible interpretations that even some of the champions of ambiguity have begun to be worried by wilful readers imposing their own agenda on any text that happens to get in the way. Thus, for example, a leading deconstructionist J. Hillis Miller has lamented the recent turn in literary studies away from language and texts as such towards 'history, culture, society, politics, institutions, class and gender conditions, the social context, the material base'. Miller suggests that this turn has undermined the virtue of attempting 'to read carefully, patiently, and scrupulously, under the elementary assumption that the text being read may say something different from what one expects it to say'.[26] In a similar vein, even the pragmatist Richard Rorty reports his boredom at having to slog through an anthology of essays on Conrad's *Heart of Darkness* which included methodical readings of various sorts (psycho-analytic, reader response, feminist, deconstructionist and new historicist), none of which seemed to make any difference to the critics' self-understanding. What Rorty missed in this anthology was a reader who had been 'enraptured or destabilized by the text', a reader whose interpretative interests and purposes had actually been changed by the experience of reading Conrad's novel.[27]

Rorty's remarks are intriguing, for our purposes, because they come from a debate with Umberto Eco over the possibility of establishing limits to the proliferation of interpretations. Eco thinks that such limits can and should be established but that they cannot be established by appeals to authorial intention. He argues that we need to distinguish between the intentions of a reader who may want to use a text for their own purposes (the *intentio lectoris*) and interpretation proper, which is the attempt to discover the intentions of a text as a coherent whole (*intentio operis*). Rorty, on the other hand, thinks that the distinction is unworkable. He argues that there is no such thing as the essential content of a text which can be used as an independent standard to evaluate a reader's hypothesis. Interpretations are only coherent with respect to some particular purpose, some particular *intentio*, which a reader happens to have. Rorty stands together with Stanley Fish and Jeffrey Stout in describing what he calls 'a thoroughly pragmatic account of interpretation, one which no longer contrasts interpretation with use.[28] But even Rorty, perhaps the most extreme defender of readers' rights, thinks that readings which simply replicate critical prejudices are less valuable than life-changing readings which transform a critic's priorities. In expressing this view, he seems to be withdrawing from the prospect of readers who beat any text into the shape that suits their own purposes.[29]

I mention the debate between Rorty and Eco not so as to return to epistemological matters but as a way of raising the issue of readerly commitments. In my view, the pragmatists are right to think that the interpretation of a text is shaped by our prior interpretative interests. However, against the pragmatists, I want to insist that we need to distinguish between two basic kinds of readerly 'interest': on the one hand there are interpretative interests which are the goals of particular critical methods or strategies of reading (e.g., interests in sources, genre, intention, material conditions, reception and so on); on the other hand, there are the reader's own values, ideology, commitments or purposes. All of these might loosely be called 'interests', but one kind of interest is more directly connected to interpretation in the narrower sense, and the other kind has more to do with the uses of interpretation.

Let us take feminist biblical studies as an example. A commitment to feminism certainly produces a focus either on texts which mention women or on the history of women in the ancient world. What it does not produce is a single method or strategy of reading. Some feminist studies are primarily interested in social and economic history (e.g. Carol Meyers's book *Discovering Eve*), some in source criticism (e.g. Phyllis Bird's work on Gen. 1), and some in literary approaches to the text as such (e.g. Phyllis Trible in *Texts of Terror*).[30] Strictly speaking, there is probably no such thing as a distinctive feminist criticism; rather, there are a variety of methods and strategies which have been adopted by readers with emancipatory commitments.

Feminism is distinctive in its use of women's experience and values, but the interpretative methods used by feminists are shared with others who are not feminists. Thus, as far as method is concerned, there is a deep continuity between Meyer's *Discovering Eve*, Norman Gottwald's *The Tribes of Yahweh*, Niels Lemche's *Early Israel*, and Itumeleng Mosala's *Biblical Hermeneutics and Black Theology in South Africa*. Of these books, only *Discovering Eve* has a primary commitment to feminism, and I would argue, therefore, that a distinction arises here between 'interpretative interests' which guide a particular method, and interests in the broader sense of ethical commitments and purposes.[31] Meyers is able to describe the changing position of women throughout Israelite history, but her evaluative preference is for the pre-monarchic period; during this period the oppression of women was apparently less evident. Similarly, Bird follows in the long tradition of source criticism in her narrowly *interpretative* interest in describing the Priestly intention of Gen. 1, but her *ethical* interest arises when she judges that intention to be androcentric.

But having defended this distinction between interpretation and use, I also want to defend those committed readers who have chastised the guilds of biblical criticism for making a virtue out of suppressing ethical commitments. Biblical critics have no less of a social responsibility than any other specialist. What we need is more discussion of how to express that responsibility, and the contributions of committed readers – whether feminist, or liberationist, or ecological, etc. – are to be welcomed. Some may fear that this simply opens the floodgates to all kinds of ideology (a fear which seems to presume an unproblematic distinction between ideological and non-ideological criticism), but there are at least two points to be made against such a response. First, the only alternative seems to be a retreat into scholarship as pure contemplation, and such a retreat is probably illusory. At the very least, scholarship is often driven by motives like the advancement of a career, and in such cases, the ethical choice seems to be between personal advancement and broad emancipatory commitments.[32]

Second, I want to suggest that precisely because there is a difference between ethical purposes and interpretative method, the implicit or explicit ideology of any particular reading can always be brought into dialogue with others who use the same method but who have other commitments.[33] Feminist, liberationist, and ecological studies of the Bible are not advancing distinctive methods, and in this sense, they are not directly comparable with, say, source criticism or formalism.[34] Ethical concerns might well influence the interpretations that particular critics offer, but precisely because committed readers use methods in the public domain there are limits to interpretation which are imposed by that public context of discussion. Consequently, I suspect that biblical studies as a discipline has very little to fear from ideologically committed readings, and a lot to gain. Ideology will always be a feature of research, and it is only dangerous when it hides itself and denies the possibility of critique from outsiders.

In conclusion, one would need to say that reader theory is too diverse a phenomenon to treat under one heading. We should stop alluding to it as if it were a homogeneous block of thinking that can either be swallowed whole or summarily dismissed. Certain versions of reader criticism are essentially contributions to epistemology and only make a difference at that level. They tend to repeat the point that was made long ago, namely, that exegesis always has presuppositions. But the interesting question is not *whether* exegesis has presuppositions, but rather, what *kinds* of presuppositions –

whether epistemological, methodological, ideological, and so on. Finally, it may be that the return of the reader will allow us to regain that great tradition which was shared by both Reformation and Enlightenment exegetes, namely, the tradition of reading the Bible in the service of social and religious reform.

Notes

1. See the remarks on the former US Secretary of Education William Bennett, in H. Aram Veeser (ed.), *The New Historicism*, London: Routledge 1989, 28.
2. See, e.g., M.G. Brett 'Motives and Intentions in Genesis 1', *Journal of Theological Studies* 42/1 (1991), 1–16; S.R. Suleiman 'Introduction: Varieties of Audience-Oriented Criticism' in: S.R. Suleiman and I. Crosman (eds), *The Reader in the Text*, Princeton: Princeton University Press 1981, 3–45.
3. For the time scale of three decades see D. Clines, *What Does Eve Do to Help?*, Sheffield: Sheffield Academic Press 1991, 9–12; contrast S. Moore, *Literary Criticism and the Gospels*, New Haven: Yale University Press 1989, 73: 'each new stage has tended less to displace the previous one than simply to be superimposed on it'.
4. S. Fish, *Is There a Text in this Class?*, Cambridge, Mass.: Harvard University Press 1980, 163; E. Conrad, *Reading Isaiah*, Philadelphia: Fortress Press 1991, 4.
5. See S. Fish, *Doing What Comes Naturally*, Oxford: Clarendon 1989, 15, 98–100. Note that Fish rejects any notion of an intention which is somehow separable from the meaning of a text, arguing that intentionality is essentially 'conventional behaviour' (pp. 98–100). This view, it seems to me, fails to distinguish between motives and communicative intentions. The whole point of a lie, for example, is that a speaker's deeper intent is detachable from his or her linguistic meaning. See further Brett, 'Motives and Intentions in Genesis 1' (n. 2 above).
6. Fish, *Doing*, 116–17.
7. Indeed, Stanley Porter even seems to think that unless New Testament critics accept Fish's notion of an interpretative community, they will not produce any genuine examples of reader-response criticism. 'Why Hasn't Reader-Response Criticism Caught on in New Testament Studies?' *Journal of Literature and Theology* 4 (1990), 287.
8. Fish, *Doing*, 116–17; similarly, I. Maclean 'Reading and Interpretation', in A. Jefferson and D. Robey (eds), *Modern Literary Theory*, London: B.T. Batsford 1986, 122–44. After reviewing the philosophical

contributions of Ingarden and Gadamer, Maclean suggests that they 'do more to justify and describe the process of reading than to provide models for critical practice' (143).

9. As a narrative unfolds, the reader constantly evaluates a character within the story with respect to what that character thus far knows. Thus, characterization, point of view, and sequential reading are all integrally related. In biblical books, however, the matter is often complicated by the fact that the reader is given additional information that characters within the story do not have, e.g., when we are told at the beginning of Job that what is about to transpire is a divine test. Sequential reading then becomes a process of comparing the reader's point of view with the various characters' points of view as they develop. See further A. Berlin, *Poetics and Interpretation of Biblical Narrative*, Sheffield: Almond Press 1983, ch. 3; M. Sternberg, *Poetics of Biblical Narrative*, Bloomington: Indiana University Press 1985, ch. 4.

10. R. Fowler, *Loaves and Fishes*, Chico: Scholars Press 1981, 140–41.

11. W. Iser, 'Indeterminacy and the Reader's Response in Prose Fiction' in: J. Hillis Miller (ed.), *Aspects of Narrative*, New York: Columbia University Press 1971, 1–45. Reprinted in W. Iser, *Prospecting: From Reader Response to Literary Anthropology*, London: John Hopkins 1989, ch. 1.

12. See note 11 and H.R. Jauss, 'The Theory of Reception: A Retrospective of its Unrecognized Prehistory' in P. Collier and H. Geyer-Ryan (eds), *Literary Theory Today*, Oxford: Polity Press 1990, 59. For an encyclopaedic example of the study of reception see H. von Erffa, *Ikonologie der Genesis* Band 1, Munich: Deutscher Kunstverlag 1989.

13. Clines, *What Does Eve Do to Help?* chs 1–3; W.S. Vorster 'Readings, Readers and the Succession Narrative' *Zeitschrift für die alttestamentliche Wissenschaft* 98 (1986), 351–62.

14. S. Fish, *Is There a Text in this Class?* 7.

15. It is only the early Fish who delivers anything of methodological significance, and he still sees some pedagogical value in the strategy of chronological reading despite its philosophical naivety'. See *Text*, 22.

16. D. Gunn, 'Reading Right' in: D. Clines, S. Fowl, S. Porter (eds), *The Bible in Three Dimensions*, Sheffield: Sheffield Academic Press 1990, 62.

17. E.g. F. Lentricchia, *After the New Criticism*, Chicago: University of Chicago Press 1980, 180.

18. M. Fishbane, *Biblical Interpretation in Ancient Israel*, Oxford: Oxford University Press 1985; J. Barton, *Oracles of God*, London: Darton, Longman & Todd 1986.

19. To mention one extreme example, I have elsewhere suggested that already in 1895 Gunkel had provided a reading of Gen. 1 which was, in some respects, deconstructionist. See Brett, 'Motives and Intentions', 3;

cf. the editors' introduction to M. Worton and J. Still (eds), *Inter-textuality*, Manchester: Manchester University Press 1990, 1–44.

20. H.R. Jauss, *Toward an Aesthetic of Reception*, Brighton: Harvester Press 1982, 28. See further M.G. Brett, *Biblical Criticism in Crisis?*, Cambridge: Cambridge University Press 1991, 127–34.

21. J. Barton, *Amos's Oracles Against the Nations*, Cambridge: Cambridge University Press 1980, 3.

22. Ibid., 3–4, 46–50.

23. See, e.g., S.R. Suleiman, 'Introduction', 8–9; D. Rhoads and D. Michie, *Mark as Story*, Philadelphia: Fortress Press 1982, 137.

24. Cf. J. Culler, *On Deconstruction*, Ithaca: Cornell University Press 1982, 66–71; Moore, *Literary Criticism*, 92 n. 29, and 95.

25. W. Ong 'Text as Interpretation: Mark and After' *Semeia* 39 (1987), 22; Moore, *Literary Criticism*, 84–88.

26. J. Hillis Miller, 'Presidential Address 1986. The Triumph of Theory, the Resistance to Reading, and the Question of Material Base' *PMLA* 102 (1987), 283.

27. R. Rorty, 'The Pragmatist's Progress' in U. Eco et al., *Interpretation and Overinterpretation*, Cambridge: Cambridge University Press 1992, 106–7.

28. Ibid., 98–101. Cf. J. Stout 'What is the Meaning of a Text' *NLH* 14/1 (1982), 1–12.

29. R. Rorty, *Consequences of Pragmatism*, Minneapolis: University of Minnesota Press 1982, 151.

30. C. Meyers, *Discovering Eve*, Oxford: Oxford University Press 1988; P. Bird, 'Male and Female He Created Them', *Harvard Theological Review* 74 (1981), 129–59; P. Trible *Texts of Terror*, Philadelphia: Fortress Press 1984; London: SCM Press 1992.

31. N. Gottwald, *The Tribes of Yahweh*, Maryknoll: Orbis and London: SCM Press 1979; N. Lemche, *Early Israel* SVT 37, Leiden: Brill 1985; I. Mosala, *Biblical Hermeneutics and Black Theology in South Africa*, Grand Rapids: Eerdmans 1989. I am not meaning to deny that some authors see a direct connection between their method and their ethics; particular interpretative interests can and should be given ethical defences. The point here is simply that a method is not, in itself, an ethic.

32. I should concede that 'pure contemplation' may be governed by an ethic that is not simply self-serving. E.g., a purely descriptive interest in authorial intentions might lay claim to a Kantian ethic which suggests that authors should be respected as ends in themselves and not simply manipulated for one's own purposes. Such a defence of intentionalist criticism would, however, be simplistic if it failed to address considerations which might conflict with this all-too-convenient application of Kant. For example, the motive or intention of an ancient author may

have been to suppress the views of others who should equally be regarded as ends in themselves. Futher, such a defence of intentionalist criticism would be incomplete if it failed to address the ethical context of the interpreter as well (e.g., where the interpreter is located within elite institutions with the resources and rewards which support scholarly interests in great, dead authors).

33. E.g., we have recently witnessed a dispute between David Gunn and Meir Sternberg over the question of readerly ideology. Precisely because they use the same kind of interpretative method which focusses primarily on texts in their final form, Gunn and Sternberg have been able to begin a mutually critical dialogue about how ideological factors have influenced their respective readings. See note 16, and D. Fewell and D. Gunn 'Tipping the Balance: Sternberg's Reader and the Rape of Dinah' *Journal of Biblical Literature* 110/2 (1991), 193–211, esp. 211.

34. Cf. G. West, *Biblical Hermeneutics of Liberation: Modes of Reading the Bible in the South African Context*, Pietermaritzburg: Cluster Publications, 1991. This book strongly argues that biblical scholars should have emancipatory commitments, but it also demonstrates that no one method or 'mode of reading' is uniquely suited to such commitments.

2

Treasures Old and New: Biblical Theology and the Challenge of Feminism

Phyllis Trible

Biblical faith embraces treasures old and new (Matt. 13.52). This image captures the purpose of our essay: to initiate a conversation between an old treasure called biblical theology and a new one called feminist hermeneutics. At first glance, the two topics seem far removed from each other; at second glance, they appear perpetual enemies. A third look, however, shows that they can meet, wrestle together, and then effect a blessing.[1]

A Sketch of Biblical Theology

Not unlike other disciplines, biblical theology is a flawed treasure. Though belonging historically to a circumscribed community, its practitioners have never agreed on definition, method, organization, subject matter, point of view, or purpose of their enterprise.

1. From the beginnings to 1933

Drawing upon earlier studies, Johann Philipp Gabler formulated the discipline in the late eighteenth century (1787) for the European world, particularly the German scene.[2] He deemed it a historical and descriptive task distinct from the didactic and interpretive goal of dogmatic theology. At the same time, he related the two fields by making biblical theology the foundation of dogmatics.

For about a century afterwards the discipline flourished in disputation. Even the label 'biblical theology' became suspect. The idea of a single scripture contrasted with the view of separated parts. So the term 'Old Testament theology' emerged to specify a Christian bias that not infrequently disparaged the subject. Interpretive approaches contended with descriptive. Searches for unifying themes brought disunity. The concepts 'universal' and 'unique' vied for supremacy in determining subject matter and point of view. And debate about organization opposed chronologies of biblical content to categories of systematic theology.

From Europe the discussion entered the English speaking world largely through the work of A.B. Davidson (1831–1892) of New College Edinburgh.[3] Edited posthumously, this theology drew upon six different versions, all unfinished. They attested to the ongoing conflict about method and content. Before the end of the nineteenth century, then, biblical theology, though dominated by a circumscribed community, had developed in myriad ways, often incompatible.

Thereupon followed forty years of wilderness wanderings (*c.* 1880–1920). Emphasis on the history of religions threatened the discipline by promoting cultural rather than theological concerns. By the mid-1920s, interest revived. Two articles represented the shift. Otto Eissfeldt argued for the legitimacy yet discontinuity of historical and theological approaches to the Old Testament.[4] By contrast, Walther Eichrodt maintained that an irreconcilable separation between these two approaches was neither possible nor desirable.[5] He rejected Eissfeldt's definition of Old Testament theology as solely normative and interpretive. Like Gabler, he defined it as predominately descriptive and historical, even while acknowledging a role for faith in its composition.

2. From 1933 to 1960

In 1933, when Germany came under National Socialist control, Eichrodt produced in Basel the first volume of his theology, with the second and third to follow in 1935 and 1939.[6] He himself made no hermeneutical connection with his own setting. Rather, he described the discipline as giving 'a complete picture of the Old Testament realm of belief'. This picture formed the centre panel of a triptych. On one side, the religions of the ancient Near East showed comparatively the uniqueness of the Old Testament. On the other, the New Testament produced a theological union through the concept 'kingdom of God'. Judaism Eichrodt denigrated. A 'systematic synthesis' defined his method. Of the organizing categories – God and the People, God and the World, God and Humankind (*Mensch*) – the first was basic. Covenant constituted its symbol. Though largely a product of nineteenth-century thought, Eichrodt's formulation dominated biblical theology into the latter half of the twentieth century.

Quite a different paradigm emerged in the work of Gerhard von Rad.[7] Volume 1 of his theology appeared in 1957, a little over a decade after World War II; volume 2 followed three years later. Like Eichrodt, von Rad made no connection with his own historical and political setting. Form criticism and tradition history shaped his method. Rather than positing a centre (*Mitte*) for biblical theology or using systematic categories, he appealed to Israel's own testimonies about divine activity in history. The first volume interpreted the Hexateuch, the Deuteronomistic History, and the Chronicler's History to conclude with Israel's response in the Psalter and the Wisdom literature. The second volume studied prophecy as God's 'new thing' in the land. A brief look at apocalypticism led to the final section, tracing the Old Testament into the New. Von Rad declared this movement the *sine qua non* of the enterprise. Without it, one had instead the 'history of the religion of the Old Testament'.

If Eichrodt be the *'aleph*, then von Rad is the *taw* of an extraordinary period in the history of biblical theology. During this time white male European Protestant scholars controlled the subject. Their power extended wherever the discipline was taught. In Great Britain the names of H.H. Rowley, C.H. Dodd, Norman H. Snaith, Norman Porteous, and the like come to mind. In the United States James Muilenburg, James D. Smart, and Bernhard W. Anderson shaped the agenda but perhaps most significantly, George Ernest Wright. Influenced by both Eichrodt and von Rad, he argued for biblical theology as recital of God's activity in history.[8]

3. From 1960 to the Present

Yet the mighty consensus (at least, presumed) fell, eroded by factors extrinsic and intrinsic. Reporting the story, Brevard Childs cites *Honest to God* by the British New Testament scholar J.A.T. Robinson as one of several publications that exposed the flaws and sought new directions.[9] For our purposes, the 1963 date of this publication is uncanny. That same year in the United States a Jewish housewife named Betty Friedan produced *The Feminine Mystique*.[10] Her book marked the beginning of the so-called 'second wave' of feminism on the American scene. Five years later (1968) Mary Daly became the first religious voice on the subject.[11] The waning of a major period in biblical theology and the waxing of feminism in American consciousness converged in time. A feminist biblical scholar does not let this convergence go unnoticed. In the decade of the 60s treasures old and new came under scrutiny.

Since 1963 few biblical theologies have appeared, and none has dominated the field. Two publications from 1978 merit note. In England Ronald Clements proposed 'a fresh approach'.[12] Christian, Jewish, and Islamic perspectives as well as attitudes toward other religions set the context for his exploration. In the United States Samuel Terrien spanned the Testaments with a unified theology of the elusive presence of God.[13] Seven years later (1985) he produced a theology of manhood and womanhood, seemingly an effort to engage feminism.[14] In that same year Childs set the discipline within a canonical context. A brief discussion entitled 'Male and Female As A Theological Problem' spurned feminist analysis.[15] Overall, these three male scholars saw biblical theology in transition. While each employed the adjective *new* to describe the need of the present, his own offering resonated more with the old.[16]

4. *Characteristics and challenges*

Of various characteristics that have marked biblical theology throughout its two hundred year history (1787–1992), four bear upon our topic. First, practitioners have struggled without resolution to define method and content.[17] Over time their discussion has acquired the status of *déjà dit*. Proposals and counterproposals but repeat themselves. Second, guardians of the discipline have fitted a standard profile. They have been white Christian males from Europe, Britain, or North America, educated in seminaries, divinity schools, or theological faculties. Third, their interpretations have skewed or neglected matters not congenial to an androcentric point of view. Fourth, they have fashioned biblical theology in a past separated from the present. They have kept the discipline apart from biblical hermeneutics.[18]

Challenges now come from many directions. Spurred by Latin American thinkers, liberation theologies foster redefinition and seek appropriation.[19] Sociological and literary analyses bring further insights as do racial, ethnic, and sexual perspectives.[20] Africans, African-Americans, Asians, Jews, and others shape the discipline differently from traditional proponents.[21] Issues such as ecology, medical ethics, creationism, and spirituality also press for dialogue. In short, biblical theology endures to grapple with hermeneutics. Such expanding horizons lead us to the feminist challenge.

Feminist Study of the Bible

1. Point of departure

Joining biblical studies in the early 1970s, feminism has introduced an interpretive stance that counters traditional thinking.[22] Though far from monolithic in point of view, it focusses on gender and sex: masculine and feminine roles as culturally perceived and biological distinctions between male and female.[23] Historically, societies have used gender and sex to advocate male domination and female subordination. The term 'sexism' denotes this ideology. It fosters a system called patriarchy. Acquiring a definition beyond classical law, the word 'patriarchy' describes the institutionalization of male dominance over women in home and in society at large. Male authority does not necessarily imply that women have no power or that all women are victims. Its impact may be subtle as well as blatant. To identify sexism and patriarchy constitutes one task of feminism.

Another task convicts. It opposes the paradigm of domination and subordination in all forms, particularly male over female, but also master over slave, rich over poor, and humankind over the earth. Sex, race, class, and ecology intertwine. Yet a third task seeks a healing vision for humankind. Its goal is wholeness and well-being, specifically gender redemption. In pursuing these tasks, feminism becomes a prophetic movement. It examines the *status quo*, pronounces judgment, and calls for repentance.[24]

The designation 'prophetic' engenders several observations. First, by definition, prophetic movements advocate.[25] This activity neither distinguishes nor demeans feminism but rather characterizes all theologies and methods. For centuries church, synagogue, and academy have advocated patriarchy as the way things are and ought to be. In exposing their bias, feminism evokes a different hermeneutic. Second, as the generic term 'prophecy' covers multiple perspectives, so the generic 'feminism' embraces plurality and diversity. Time, place, culture, class, race, experience – these and other variables yield particular expressions of a shared interest. Third, though particularities induce conflict and contradiction, they also serve as self-critical reflection. Feminism grapples with the awareness that prophetic movements are not themselves exempt from sin. Jewish feminist theology, for example, detects anti-Jewish sentiments in some Christian formulations.[26] Third World feminists criticize the privileged positions of class and race that afflict First World feminism.[27] African-American women, claiming the identity 'womanist', challenge white feminists.[28] On individual levels experiences of women differ to yield diverse witnesses. While announcing judgment on patriarchy and calling for repentance, feminism struggles with its own sins.

2. An initial approach

When feminism studies the Bible, it names the sin of patriarchy. A summary picture of the female in ancient Israel illustrates the point. Less desirable in the eyes of her parents than a male child, a girl stayed close to her mother, but her father controlled her life until he relinquished her to another man for marriage. If either of these male authorities permitted her to be mistreated, even abused, she had to submit without recourse. Thus Lot offered his daughters to the men of Sodom to protect a male guest (Gen. 19.8); Jephthah sacrificed his daughter to remain faithful to a foolish vow (Judg. 11.29–40); Amnon raped his half-sister Tamar (II Sam. 13); and the Levite from the hill country of Ephraim participated with other males to bring about the betrayal, rape, torture, murder, and dismemberment of his own concubine (Judg. 19). Although not every story involving female and male is so terrifying, nevertheless, the narrative literature makes clear that from birth to death the Hebrew woman belonged to men.

What such narratives show, the legal corpus amplifies. Defined as the property of men (Ex. 20.17; Deut. 5.21), women did not control their own bodies. A man expected to marry a virgin, though his own virginity need not be intact. A wife found guilty of earlier fornication was deemed to have violated the honour and power of both her father and husband. Death by stoning was the penalty (Deut.

The Open Text

22.13–21). According to the law, a woman had no right to divorce (Deut. 24.1–4) and, most often, no right to own property. Excluded from the priesthood, she was considered more unclean than the male (Lev. 15), and her monetary value was less (Lev. 27.1–7).

Evidence for the subordination, inferiority, and abuse of women abounds in scripture. Feminism has no difficulty making this case and thus convicting the Bible of the sin of patriarchy. Yet the conviction has led to different conclusions. Some feminists denounce scripture as hopelessly misogynous, a woman-hating document with no health in it.[29] Some reprehensibly use these patriarchal data to support anti-Jewish sentiments. They maintain that ascendancy of the male god Yahweh demolished an era of good-goddess worship.[30] A Christian version holds that whereas the 'Old' Testament falters badly, the 'New' brings improved revelation.[31] Some feminists consider the Bible to be a historical document devoid of continuing authority and hence worthy of dismissal. By contrast, others despair about the ever-present male power that the Bible and its commentators hold over women. And still others, unwilling to let the case against women be the determining word, insist that text and interpreters provide more excellent ways.[32] They seek a new biblical theology, one that redeems the past (an ancient treasure called the Bible) and the present (its continuing use) from the confines of patriarchy. During the last fifteen years or so, some of these responses have joined scholarly study of the Bible.[33]

3. Samplings of feminist biblical scholarship

Whatever their conclusions, feminist biblical scholars use conventional methods to study the text. Historical criticism, form criticism, tradition history, literary criticism, sociology, anthropology, archaeology, history of religions, and linguistics – all these and others contribute to theological formulations. Traditionally tied to patriarchal interpretation, the methods now produce different results. Our sampling comes from scholars in the United States.

Working as a historical critic, Phyllis Bird has called for 'a new reconstruction of the history of Israelite religion, not a new chapter on women' within a traditional framework. A first step seeks to recover 'the hidden history of women'. She has contributed to this immense task several articles examining women in ancient Israel and in the Israelite cult.[34] Similarly, Jo Ann Hackett locates her research in 'the new women's history'.[35] It attempts to recover the stories of females in their own right rather than measuring them by the norms of male history. In an examination of Judges 3–16, for instance, Hackett explores the leadership roles of women during a period of decentralized power. Paucity of evidence, difficulty of analysis, and resistance from established scholarship lead her to a pessimistic assessment about the impact of such work on so-called mainline thinking.

More sanguine about the possibilities, Carol Meyers has written the first book-length study of Israelite women. Using the tools of social-scientific analysis combined with the new archaeology, she seeks 'the place of women in the biblical world apart from the place of women in the biblical text'. She questions the validity of the description 'patriarchal' for ancient Israelite society to argue that 'the decentralized and difficult village life of premonarchic Israel provided a context for gender mutuality and interdependence, and of concomitant female power'. In subsequent centuries this parity eroded significantly, even though qualifying influences continued until the late pre-exilic period.[36]

Cheryl Exum[37] and Toni Craven[38] have employed literary critical analysis in their feminist exegesis. While acknowledging the dominant patriarchal stance of scripture, they ferret out counter pictures through the method of close reading: e.g., the women of the Exodus and the books of Ruth, Esther, and Judith. These and other literary readings provide an exegetical base for theological reflection.

Scholarly work on wisdom literature also provides data for the theologian. Combining several methods, historical, sociological, and literary, Claudia Camp has explored female wisdom in Proverbs.[39] Viewing 'woman Wisdom' as metaphor, she has isolated roles and activities within Israelite culture that influenced this personification. They include the figures of wife, lover, harlot, foreigner, prophet, and wise woman.

Investigating Israelite law, Tikva Frymer-Kensky has studied such cases as the trial of the suspected adulterer in Num. 5.11–31.[40] She has also tackled the large question of how the Bible treats sex, arguing that appreciation and anxiety vie without a way to channel the latter productively. 'The result is a core emptiness in the Bible's discussion of sex.'[41] Her research draws heavily upon ancient Near Eastern religions and philological and linguistic data. Most importantly, she has contributed a major study on goddesses as they relate to the radical monotheistic agenda of the Bible and to the current, often ill-informed and uninformed, interest in 'the Goddess'.[42] Reliable scholarship blends historical description and interpretive analysis, a combination congenial to theological pursuits.

These samplings conclude with three books that differ widely in interest, approach, and purpose but share a common grounding. Particular experiences motivated their authors. Unlike traditional male scholars, feminists often spell out hermeneutical connections between life and work. Citing an episode within her Jewish heritage as pertinent to her study, Athalya Brenner probes the familiar thesis that, as a class, women in scripture are a second sex, always subordinate and sometimes maligned.[43] Her approach covers social roles and literary paradigms. Writing as a womanist, Renita J. Weems 'attempts to combine the best of the fruits of feminist biblical criticism with its passion for reclaiming and reconstructing the stories of biblical women, along with the best of the Afro-American oral tradition, with its gift for story-telling and its love of drama'.[44] Recounting unpleasant experiences within Roman Catholicism, Alice L. Laffey has prepared a 'complement' to standard introductions of the Old Testament.[45] She interprets texts, for weal or woe, on the principle 'that women are equal to men'. However scholarly judgments measure these works, the experiences that prompted their authors and the methods they employ affect theological discourse.

Not surprisingly, the research of feminist biblical scholars contrasts with patriarchal scholarship from the past to the present. Thereby they help to identify and relativize the latter. They also show the impossibility of methodological neutrality or objectivity. Perspective shapes method, no matter how much the protest. Studying the Bible from the viewpoint of gender and sex, feminists explore ideas, discover data, and advance theses shunned in traditional interpretations. Conventional methods produce unconventional results. As with patriarchal scholarship, not all feminist points of view agree and not all will endure. Yet the ferment is salutary, for the storehouse of faith has treasures new as well as old. They necessitate the perennial rethinking of biblical theology.[46]

Overtures to Feminist Biblical Theology

As a student of scripture, I read biblical theology from duty and sometimes delight. As a student of feminism, I read feminist scholarship from duty and sometimes delight. And then I ask: Can feminism and biblical theology meet? The question seems to echo Tertullian, 'What has Athens to do with Jerusalem?' After all, feminists do not move in the world of Gabler, Eichrodt, von Rad, and their heirs. Yet feminists who love the Bible insist that the text and its interpreters provide more excellent ways. And so I ponder ingredients of a feminist biblical theology. Though not yet the season to write one, the time has come to make overtures.

At the beginning, feminist biblical theology might locate itself with reference to the classical discipline. Assertion without argumentation suffices here. First, the undertaking is not just descriptive and historical but primarily constructive and hermeneutical. It views the Bible as pilgrim, wandering through history, engaging in new settings, and ever refusing to be locked in the past. Distance and difference engage proximity and familiarity.[47] Second, the discipline belongs to diverse communities, including academy, synagogue, church, and world. It is neither essentially nor necessarily Christian. Third, formulations vary. No single method, organization, or exposition harnesses the subject: an articulation of faith as disclosed in scripture.

From these points of reference feminism takes its first step toward biblical theology, namely exegesis. It focusses on reinterpreting familiar texts and highlighting neglected ones. Two passages from Genesis provide soundings.

1. Exegesis: Eve and Adam

Throughout the ages theologians have used this most familiar of all texts, the story of the Garden in Genesis 2–3, to legitimate patriarchy as the will of God.[48] So powerful has been this interpretation that it has burrowed its way into the collective psyche of the Western world. Among major contentions appear the following: man is created first and woman last; this order of creation makes her subordinate to him; she derives from his side; she becomes his helper, his assistant, not his equal; she seduces him into disobedience; she is cursed and then punished by being explicitly subjected to the rule of her husband.

Over against this misogynous reading feminism sets a counter exegesis. It begins with the making of a pun, the forming of *hā-'ādām* dust from *hā-'adāmâ*. The definite article *hā-* preceding the common

41

noun *'ādām* indicates the generic rather than the particular. The pun resulting from linkage with the corresponding word *hā-'adāmâ* becomes in English 'the human from the humus'. Other than references to dust and nostrils, the description of the human remains sparse. Most importantly, it is not sexually identified as the male or 'the first man'. Man the male enters the story only with the advent of woman the female. And that happens at the end of chapter 2. By divine surgery the one human from the humus becomes two, female and male, in the sexually explicit vocabulary *'iššâ* and *'îš*. These two are bone of bones and flesh of flesh, the language of mutuality and equality. Thus Yhwh God does not create the primal woman second to the primal man.

Moreover, she is not his 'helper', his subordinate, his assistant, his inferior. Overwhelmingly in scripture the Hebrew word *'ēzer'*, traditionally translated 'helper', describes God as the superior one who creates and saves Israel.[49] (So if we have trouble with this word, it is not the trouble we thought we had.) In the Garden story the phrase accompanying *''ēzer'*, namely 'fit for' or 'corresponding to', (*kᵉnegdô*) tempers the connotation of superiority to specify mutuality and companionship.

The woman called Eve is not 'Adam's rib'. That rib or side (which belongs anyway to the sexually undifferentiated first creature) constitutes but raw material requiring further divine activity. God takes the material and 'builds it into woman'. The Hebrew verb *build* (*bnh*) indicates considerable labour to produce solid and lasting results. It constructs towns, towers, altars, and fortifications. Hence, the primal woman appears as no weak, dainty, ephemeral creature. Instead, she is the culmination of the story, fulfilling humanity in sexuality. Though equal in creation with the man, she becomes elevated in emphasis by the design of the narrative. 'Therefore, a man leaves his father and his mother and cleaves to his woman and they become one flesh' (Gen. 2.24). In this description only the man has parental identity; the woman stands alone. Her independence as a human creature remains intact.

In Genesis 3 the serpent addresses the woman with plural verb forms, thereby rendering her spokesperson for the human couple (hardly the pattern of patriarchal culture). 'Did God say, "You shall not eat of any fruit...?"' he asked. To answer his question, the woman states the case for obedience even more strongly than did God. She maintains, 'From the fruit of the tree that is in the midst of the Garden, God said, "You shall not eat from it and you shall not touch it, lest you die"' (Gen. 3.2–3). This quotation embellishes the divine words with the phrase, 'you shall not touch it'. The woman's interpretive skills emerge. Her understanding guarantees obedience. If the tree is not touched, then its fruit cannot be eaten. Thus she builds 'a fence around Torah', a procedure that her rabbinical successors have developed fully to protect the law of God and ensure obedience. Speaking with clarity and authority, Eve is theologian, ethicist, hermeneut, rabbi, and preacher. By contrast, the man *who was with her* (a telling phrase that many translations over centuries have omitted) appears mindless and mute. His one act is belly-oriented: 'and he ate' (Gen. 3.6).

Disobedience shatters the created mutuality of the sexes. The man betrays the woman and blames God for putting her in the Garden. In the ensuing judgments, God's words to the woman require careful exegesis. 'Your desire is for your man but he rules over you' (Gen. 3.16). Contrary to conventional interpretation, these words do not proclaim male dominance and female subordination as the will of God. They do not characterize creation nor prescribe human relationships. Instead, they describe life after disobedience, with patriarchy as one of its manifestations. Disobedience leads to expulsion from the Garden.

Overall, the story of the Garden shows us who we are, creatures of mutuality and equality, and who we have become, creatures of oppression. And so it opens possibilities for change, for a return to our true creaturehood under God. In other words, the story calls upon female and male to repent. A feminist biblical theology seeks a redemptive appropriation of this story.

2. Exegesis: Sarah, Abraham, Hagar

Our second exegetical sounding comes from the so-called Abrahamic narratives (Gen. 11.27–25.10). When Eichrodt and von Rad study this material, they see only the mighty patriarch Abraham, symbol of covenant and promise.[50] Likewise, when Terrien discusses the epiphanies that punctuate these narratives, he writes solely of visitations to Abraham.[51] Yet the entire story pivots on two women, Sarah and Hagar. What male theologians miss or dismiss, the narrator (even the patriarchal narrator) shapes with acute sensitivity.[52]

In the genealogical preface Sarai receives special attention. There appear the ominous words, 'Sarai is barren; she has no child' (11.30) and also the teasing information that she, a lone woman, accompanies her husband Abram and other males from Ur to Haran. This woman threatens the demise of genealogy. The preface then stops and the call of Abram begins (12.1–3).

When Abram and his entourage reach the promised land, the Lord assures him descendants without taking account of Sarai's condition. Tension lurks. When famine sends the group to Egypt, the tension builds. Speaking for the first time ever, Abram addresses Sarai. With flattery he manipulates her. He disowns her as his wife, gives her to Pharaoh, and thereby ensures his own survival, even his prospering. For her sake Pharaoh dealt well with Abram, but also for her sake the Lord afflicted Pharaoh. In the end, the monarch reprimands Abram and holds him accountable for the use of his wife. Pharaoh respects another man's property. Throughout it all, Sarai has neither voice nor choice. Though she remains central in the episode, patriarchy marginalizes this manhandled woman.

The story continues with a telling comment by the narrator. 'Now Sarai, wife of Abram, did not bear a child to him, but to her was an Egyptian maid whose name was Hagar' (16.1). Beginning with Sarai and ending with Hagar, this sentence contrasts two women around the man Abram. Sarai the Hebrew is married, rich, and free but also old and barren. Hagar the Egyptian is single, poor, and slave; she is also young and fertile. Power belongs to Sarai, the subject of action; powerlessness marks Hagar, the object. And so Sarai, speaking for the first time, proposes a plan to obtain children through Hagar. Abram consents; Hagar conceives. Inevitably the women clash. The pregnant maid sees the lowering of hierarchical barriers, and the barren mistress resents her loss of status. Reasserting power, Sarai afflicts Hagar.

Fleeing the house of bondage (even as Israel will later flee affliction by Pharaoh), this Egyptian slave escapes to the wilderness. There the messenger of God finds her by a spring of water, commands her to return to Sarai, and yet promises her innumerable descendants. Hagar is the only woman in all scripture to receive such a promise; moreover, she is the first person ever to receive a divine visitation. The epiphanic tradition of Israel originates not with Abraham but with the Egyptian slave Hagar.

Upon her return Hagar gives birth to Ishmael, but God makes

clear that only Sarai can bear the child of promise. She is the chosen, exalted vessel of blessing (17.15–16). At long last, it comes to pass. Sarah bears Isaac. Abraham names him Laughter (*Yishaq*) but Sarah interprets its meaning: 'Laughter God has made for me; all who hear will laugh for me' (21.6). If Laughter is special to Abraham, how much more to Sarah. She claims the child for herself ('for me'). After all, he is *her* one and only son.

The situation becomes intolerable: Sarah, wife of Abraham, and Hagar, wife of Abraham; Sarah, woman on a pedestal, and Hagar, woman in the gutter; Sarah, mother of Isaac, and Hagar, mother of Ishmael. Potential equality between sons counters actual inequality between their mothers. Jealousy, envy, rivalry, and malice lead Sarah, as she did before, to assert her power within patriarchal limits (21.8–21). She orders the expulsion of the slave woman and her son. Though distressed, Abraham acquiesces. He sends Hagar away. This time in the wilderness she finds no spring of water but rather a death bed for her child. Her last words grieve, 'Let me not see the death of the child'. Then she 'lifted up her voice and she wept'. But once again the messenger of God intervenes. Divine speech and action save the child, taking him into adulthood. Yet Hagar, not God, finds him a wife from the land of Egypt. In this, her last act, she secures for herself a future.

Hagar subverts biblical theology. She is the first person to experience a theophany, the only person to name the deity, the only woman to receive a divine promise of descendants, the first to hear an annunciation, and the first to weep for her dying child. Beyond these distinctions, she foreshadows Israel's pilgrimage of faith through contrast. As a slave in bondage, she flees from suffering. Yet she experiences exodus without liberation, revelation without salvation, wilderness without covenant, wanderings without land, promise without fulfilment, and unmerited exile without return. Her story turns upside down the categories of Eichrodt, von Rad, Terrien, and a host of others. Biblical theology has yet to give Hagar her due.

Correspondingly, it has failed Sarah. The tyranny of her last words endure without resolution. 'Cast out this slave woman with her son, for the son of this slave woman will not inherit with my son, with Isaac' (21.10). The stakes for faith increase when God, speaking to Abraham, sanctions the tyranny. 'Everything that Sarah says to you, heed her voice; for in Isaac will be named to you descendants' (21.12). Sarah, chosen vessel of the legitimate heir, remains secure on the pedestal that patriarchal religion has built for her. To keep her there protects her, but it also deprives her of healing and freedom. As with Hagar, so with Sarah, biblical theology has yet to come to terms.

Commentators have sometimes noted parallels between Genesis 21, the last appearances of Hagar and Sarah, and Genesis 22, the near sacrifice of Isaac. In the wilderness with his mother Hagar, Ishmael comes close to death; a messenger of God intervenes to save him. On the mountain with his father Abraham, Isaac comes close to death; a messenger of God intervenes to save him. Thus the two sons and the divine representatives form identical pairs. The two parents, however, form a mixed pair, the female Hagar and the male Abraham. Yet Genesis 21 shows the proper contrast to be Hagar and Sarah (not Hagar and Abraham). Further, the words of Sarah foreshadow the language of chapter 22. She speaks of 'my son Isaac', a possessive formulation that Abraham has never used. And indeed Sarah's alone is the single, unqualified attachment to Isaac. After all, Abraham has 'his son Ishmael' (21.11–12) as well as 'his son Isaac' (21.4,5). Who of the two, then, Abraham or Sarah, is the appropriate character to hear the dread command, 'Take your son, your only son Isaac whom you love, and offer him as a sacrifice …' (22.1)?

Given the unique status of Sarah and her exclusive relationship to Isaac, she, not Abraham, ought to have been tested. The dynamic of the entire saga, from its genealogical preface on, requires that she appear in the climactic scene, that she learn the meaning of obedience to God, that she find liberation from possessiveness, that she free Isaac from maternal ties and so herself emerge the model of faithfulness.

Biblical patriarchy denied Sarah her story, the opportunity for healing and blessing. It excluded her and glorified Abraham. And it did not stop with these things. After securing the future of Isaac, by a substitute sacrifice and a genealogical insertion to herald his marriage with Rebekah, patriarchy had no more need for Sarah. So it eliminated her. 'Sarah lived a hundred and twenty-seven years … and Sarah died' (23.11). These words occur soon after Abraham returned from the mountain. If early on patriarchy cast out Hagar, the woman in the gutter, the time came when it also destroyed Sarah, the woman on a pedestal. Yet ironically, within the patriarchy of scripture lies the text for the redemption of Sarah. Feminist exegesis dares biblical theology to take the challenge.

3. Contours and Content

These two exegetical soundings lead to other texts as we sketch in part the contours and content of a future feminist biblical theology. First, a feminist theology would begin, as does the Bible, with creation (Gen. 1–3). It might use the phrase 'image of God male and female' as leitmotif for the entire project, relating it positively to Genesis 2 and negatively to Genesis 3.[53] Allusions to these texts would also come into play. For example, Hosea 2.16–20 appropriates the sexual vocabulary of Genesis 2 to envision a new covenant between God and Israel. It opposes two words for husband: *ba'al* the term for male domination of the female, and *'îš* the term of mutuality and equality. In the days to come, the latter will replace the former. No longer will Israel call God *ba'alî* (my lord) but rather *'îšî* (my husband in mutuality). Though this depiction keeps God male, nevertheless it disavows the hierarchical ordering of the sexes. Creation theology rewrites covenant theology. Basing a feminist biblical theology in mythical beginnings and eschatological endings contrasts what female and male are and are meant to be with what they have become. Creation theology undercuts patriarchy.

Second, from its grounding in creation, feminist theology would recover the hidden story of women. It would explore the phenomenon of gender and sex throughout scripture, attending in particular to the presence and absence of the female. Israelite religion provides one area for study. Denied full participation in the cult, some women and men probably forged an alternative Yahwism. Worship of the Queen of Heaven (Jer. 7.16–20; 44.15–28), inscriptions linking Yahweh and Asherah, and female figurines at Israelite and Judaean sites suggest a story different from the regnant one.[54] What effect does this religion have upon the character of faith? The question revives the unsettled debate about the relationship of the unique and the typical for shaping biblical theology. Probing variations between the orthodoxy of the canonical establishment and the religion of the people might bring into sharper focus the female story.[55]

Third, feminist theology would investigate language for God. While deploring the superabundance of male vocabulary, it would lift up female and feminine imagery.[56] For example, a psalmist describes God as midwife. 'Yet it was you who took me from the womb; you kept me safe on my mother's breast' (Ps. 22.9). In turn,

God becomes mother, the one upon whom the child is cast: 'On you I was cast from my birth, and since my mother bore me you have been my God' (Ps. 22.10). What this poetry suggests, Deuteronomy 32.18 makes explicit: 'You were unmindful of the Rock that bore you; you forgot the God who writhed in labor pains giving you birth.'

Hosea 11 offers another text. Verses 3–4 describe God the parent teaching Ephraim the child to walk, picking him up, and feeding him. Though patriarchal theology has long designated this imagery paternal, in ancient Israel mothers performed such tasks.[57] Claiming the imagery as maternal enhances exegesis of yet another verse. After judgment upon wayward Ephraim, God returns in compassion (vv. 8–9). A poignant outburst begins, 'How can I give you up, O Ephraim!' It concludes, 'I will not execute my fierce anger ... for I am *'ēl* and not *'îš*, the Holy One in your midst.' Innumerable translators have understood the words *'ēl* and *'îš* to contrast the divine and the human. 'For I am God and no mortal', says the NRSV.[58] Though not inaccurate, such translations miss nuances embedded in the text. Rather than using the generic *'ādām* for humanity, the poet employs the gender-specific *îš*. This vocabulary harkens back to chapter 2 where *îš*, in contrast to *ba'alî*, portrayed God as Israel's husband in mutuality. But the language kept God male. Now even that remarkable yet flawed theology deconstructs itself through denial and appeal to transcendence: 'for I am God and not a husband, the Holy One in your midst'. And the gender-specific vocabulary holds still another radical meaning: 'for I am God and not a male, the Holy One in your midst'.

This last translation makes explicit a basic affirmation needed in ancient Israel and the contemporary world. By repeatedly using male language for Yhwh, Israel risked theological misunderstanding. God is not male, and the male is not God. That Israel employed predominantly male imagery for God is, however, hardly surprising. But that it also countenanced female imagery *is* surprising. If the latter be deemed remnants of polytheism, the fact remains that nowhere does scripture prohibit them. On the contrary, they provide a needed corrective. Feminist theology would be truly biblical in exposing (male) idolatry.[59]

Fourth, feminist theology would grapple with models and meanings for authority.[60] It recognizes that, despite the word, *author*ity centres in readers. They accord a document power even as they promote the intentionality of its authors. In explicating authority, a feminist stance might appropriate a sermon from Deuteronomy (30.15–20). The Bible sets before the reader life and death, blessings and curses. Like the ancient Israelites, modern believers are commanded to choose life over death. Within this dialectic feminism can well claim the entire Bible as authoritative, though not prescriptive. Such a definition differs strikingly from traditional views of male theologians. In the interaction of text and reader, the changing of the second component alters the meaning and power of the first.

Conclusion

These tentative proposals initiate a discussion between feminism and biblical theology, with exegesis as the foundation. Though much work remains, the aim is to wrestle from the text a constructive theology for female and male. In the name of biblical integrity, this task rejects facile formulations; in the name of biblical diversity, it rejects dogmatic positions. But like Jacob wrestling at the Jabbok (Gen. 32.22–32), feminism does not let go without a blessing.

Looking at the enormity of the enterprise, critics of every persuasion might well ask, 'Why bother?' After all, Athens has nothing to do with Jerusalem. Gabler and his successors would be nonplussed, if not horrified, as would many feminists. Among abundant scriptural answers to these critics, the image of the householder remains steadfast. A feminist who loves the Bible is like a householder who brings forth out of her treasure what is new and what is old. In time that combination will yield a feminist biblical theology for the redemption of humankind.

Notes

1. This paper incorporates major sections of Phyllis Trible, 'Five Loaves and Two Fishes: Feminist Hermeneutics and Biblical Theology', *Theological Studies* 50 (1989), 279–295.
2. See J. Sandys-Wunsch and L. Eldredge, 'J.P. Gabler and the Distinction between Biblical and Dogmatic Theology: Translation, Commentary, and Discussion of His Originality', *Scottish Journal of Theology* 33 (1980), 133–58. For a history of the discipline, with ample bibliography, see J.H. Hayes and F.C. Prussner, *Old Testament Theology: Its History and Development*, Atlanta: John Knox and London: SCM Press 1985;

cf. Ronald E. Clements, 'Interpreting Old Testament Theology', *One Hundred Years of Old Testament Interpretations*, Philadelphia: The Westminster Press 1976, 118–140; John Goldingay, 'Theology (Old Testament)', *A Dictionary of Biblical Interpretation*, ed. R.J. Coggins and J.L. Houlden, London: SCM Press and Philadelphia: Trinity Press International 1990, 691–694.

3. A.B. Davidson, *Theology of the Old Testament*, ed. S.D.F. Salmond, Edinburgh: T.& T. Clark 1904.

4. O. Eissfeldt, 'Israelitisch-jüdische Religionsgeschichte und alttestamentliche Theologie', *Zeitschrift für die alttestamentliche Wissenschaft* 44 (1926), 1–12.

5. W. Eichrodt, 'Hat die alttestamentliche Theologie noch selbstständige Bedeutung innerhalb der alttestamentlichen Wissenschaft?' *Zeitschrift für die alttestamentliche Wissenschaft* 47 (1929), 83–91.

6. In English translation the three volumes became two; see W. Eichrodt, *Theology of the Old Testament*, Philadelphia: Westminster Press and Oxford: Blackwell 1961, 1967. For overview and critique, see, inter alia, Norman K. Gottwald, 'W. Eichrodt, *Theology of the Old Testament*', *Contemporary Old Testament Theologians*, ed. Robert B. Laurin, Valley Forge, PA: Judson Press 1970, 25–62.

7. For the English translation, see G. von Rad, *Old Testament Theology* (2 vols; New York: Harper & Row, and London: SCM Press 1962, 1965). For overview and critique, see G. Henton Davies, 'Gerhard von Rad, *Old Testament Theology*', *Contemporary Old Testament Theologians*, ed. Robert B. Laurin, Valley Forge, PA: Judson Press, 1970, 63–89.

8. See G. Ernest Wright, *God Who Acts: Biblical Theology as Recital*, Chicago: Henry Regnery Company 1952. For insightful critique, see esp. Landon Gilkey, 'Cosmology, Ontology, and the Travail of Biblical Language', *Journal of Religion* 41 (July, 1961) 194–205. In a later work, Wright finds Eichrodt's view 'much broader and more satisfying' than von Rad's; cf. *The Old Testament and Theology*, New York: Harper & Row 1969, 39–69.

9. Brevard S. Childs, *Biblical Theology in Crisis*, Philadelphia: The Westminster Press 1970, 85f. Cf. J.A.T. Robinson, *Honest to God*, London: SCM Press 1963.

10. Betty Friedan, *The Feminine Mystique*, New York: W.W. Norton 1963.

11. See Mary Daly, *The Church and the Second Sex*, New York: Harper & Row 1986. In an autobiographical preface to the reprinting of this book (1975), Daly disowns it, charting her 'change of consciousness from "radical Catholic" to post-christian feminist'. For a sampling a decade after Daly's work, see *Womanspirit Rising: A Feminist Reader in Religion*, ed. Carol P. Christ and Judith Plaskow, San Francisco: Harper & Row 1979.

12. Ronald E. Clements, *Old Testament Theology: A Fresh Approach*, Atlanta: John Knox Press 1978.
13. Samuel Terrien, *The Elusive Presence*, New York: Harper & Row 1978.
14. Terrien, *Till the Heart Sings*, Philadelphia: Fortress Press 1985.
15. Brevard S. Childs, *Old Testament Theology In A Canonical Context*, Philadelphia: Fortress Press 1985, esp. 88–195.
16. Other scholars seeking new directions include James A. Sanders, *From Sacred Story to Sacred Text*, Philadelphia: Fortress Press 1978; Walter Brueggemann, 'A Shape for Old Testament Theology, I: Structural Legitimation', *Catholic Biblical Quarterly* 47 (1985), 28–46; id., 'A Shape for Old Testament Theology, II: Embrace of Pain': ibid. 395–415. Cf. also Brueggemann, *Old Testament Theology: Essays in Structure, Theme, and Text*, ed. Patrick D. Miller, Jr, Minneapolis: Fortress Press, 1992.
17. See H. Graf Reventlow, 'Basic Problems in Old Testament Theology', *Journal for the Study of the Old Testament* 11 (1979), 2–22; cf. J. Barr, 'The Theological Case against Biblical Theology', in *Canon, Theology, and Old Testament Interpretation*, ed. G.M. Tucker et al., Philadelphia: Fortress 1988, 3–19.
18. For the period since 1945, see George W. Coats, 'Theology of the Hebrew Bible', in *The Hebrew Bible and Its Modern Interpreters*, ed. Douglas A. Knight and Gene M. Tucker, Philadelphia: Fortress 1985, 239–62. For a look at the past but with attention to new approaches, see John Reumann (ed.), *The Promise and Practice of Biblical Theology*, Minneapolis: Fortress Press 1991. See also Ben C. Ollenburger, Elmer A. Martens, Gerhard F. Hasel (eds), *The Flowering of Old Testament Theology: A Reader in Twentieth-Century Old Testament Theology, 1903–1990*, Winona Lake, IN: Eisenbrauns 1992.
19. See, e.g., José Porfirio Miranda, *Marx and the Bible*, Maryknoll, NY: Orbis and London: SCM Press 1974; J. Severino Croatto, *Exodus: A Hermeneutics of Freedom*, Maryknoll, NY: Orbis 1981; Elsa Tamez, *Bible of the Oppressed*, Maryknoll, NY: Orbis 1982; Willy Schottroff and Wolfgang Stegemann (eds), *God of the Lowly: Socio-Historical Interpretations of the Bible*, Maryknoll, NY: Orbis 1984; R.S. Sugirtharajah (ed.), *Voices from the Margin: Interpreting the Bible in the Third World*, London: SPCK 1991. Cf. Erhard, S. Gerstenberger, 'Der Realitätsbezug Alttestamentlicher Exegese', *Congress Volume Salamanca 1983*, ed. J.A. Emerton, Leiden: E.J. Brill 1985, 132–144. For a brief overview and critique, see Dan Cohn-Sherbok, 'Liberation Theology', *A Dictionary of Biblical Interpretation*, ed. R.J. Coggins and J.L. Houlden, London: SCM Press and Philadelphia: Trinity Press International 1990, 396–397.
20. Numerous volumes in the series entitled Overtures to Biblical Theology,

published by Fortress Press, Philadelphia and Minneapolis, from 1977 to the present and on, demonstrate aspects of the conversation. Overall, this series rejects the limitation of historical description to explore normative meanings. Distinctions between biblical theology and hermeneutics often collapse. Two recent titles illustrate the point: Sharon H. Ringe, *Jesus, Liberation, and the Biblical Jubilee: Images for Ethics and Christology* (1985), and J. Gordon Harris, *Biblical Perspectives on Aging: God and the Elderly* (1987). On the challenges posed by sociological analysis, see e.g., Norman K. Gottwald, (ed.), *The Bible and Liberation: Political and Social Hermeneutics*, Maryknoll, NY: Orbis Books 1983; David Jobling et al. (eds), *The Bible and the Politics of Exegesis*, Cleveland, OH: The Pilgrim Press 1992.

21. For an African perspective see, e.g., Itumeleng J. Mosala, *Biblical Hermeneutics and Black Theology in South Africa*, Grand Rapids, MI: W.B. Eerdmans, 1989. For African-American perspectives, see, e.g., Renita J. Weems, *Just A Sister Away: A Womanist Vision of Women's Relationships in the Bible*, San Diego, CA: LuraMedia 1988; *Interpretation for Liberation, Semeia* 47, ed. Katie Geneva Cannon and Elizabeth Schüssler Fiorenza, Atlanta: Scholars Press 1989; Cain Hope Felder, *Troubling Biblical Waters: Race, Class, and Family*, Maryknoll, NY: Orbis Books 1990; Cain Hope Felder (ed.), *Stony the Road We Trod*, Minneapolis: Fortress 1991. For Asian responses, see, e.g., Cyris H.S. Moon, *A Korean Minjung Theology: An Old Testament Perspective*, Maryknoll, NY: Orbis Books, 1985; Naim Stifan Ateek, *Justice, And Only Justice: A Palestinian Theology of Liberation*, Maryknoll, NY: 1989, 74–114. For Jewish perspectives, see J. Levenson, 'The Hebrew Bible, the Old Testament, and Historical Criticism', in *The Future of Biblical Studies*, ed. R.E. Friedman and H.G.M. Williamson, Atlanta: Scholars, 1987, 19–59; idem, 'Why Jews Are Not Interested in Biblical Theology', in *Judaic Perspectives on Ancient Israel*, ed. J. Neusner, Philadelphia: Fortress 1989, 281–307. Cf. M.H. Goshen-Gottstein, 'Tanakh Theology: The Religion of the Old Testament and the Place of Jewish Biblical Theology', in *Ancient Israelite Religion*, ed. P.D. Miller, Jr, et al., Philadelphia: Fortress 1987; also R. Rendtorff, 'Must "Biblical Theology" Be Christian Theology?', *Bible Review* 4 (1988), 40–43.

22. On the history of feminism and biblical studies in the United States, see Dorothy C. Bass, 'Women's Studies and Biblical Studies: An Historical Perspective', *Journal for the Study of the Old Testament* 22 (1982), 6–12; cf. E.W. Saunders, *Searching the Scriptures: A History of the Society of Biblical Literature 1880–1980*, Chico, Cal.: Scholars 1982. On recent developments, see Katharine Doob Sakenfeld, 'Feminist Perspectives on Bible and Theology', *Interpretation* 42 (1988), 5–18.

23. See M. Gould and R. Kern-Daniels, 'Towards a Sociological Theory of

Gender and Sex', *American Sociologist* 12(1977), 182–89. For a helpful exposition of these and other terms, see Gerda Lerner, *The Creation of Patriarchy*, New York: Oxford University Press 1986, 231–43. Cf. Rosemary Radford Ruether, 'Sexism as Ideology and Social System: Can Christianity Be Liberated from Patriarchy?' in *With Both Eyes Open: Seeing beyond Gender*, ed. P. Altenbornd Johnson and J. Kalven, New York: Pilgrim Press 1988, 148–64.

24. For substantive statements of feminist theology, see Rosemary Radford Ruether, *Sexism and God-Talk: Towards a Feminist Theology*, Boston: Beacon Press and London: SCM Press 1983; also Anne E. Carr, *Transforming Grace: Christian Tradition and Women's Experience*, San Francisco: Harper & Row 1988.

25. At places in the current discussion this point seems to be missed, with the word 'advocacy' assigned to feminism, as though it were, for better or worse, distinctive. Cf., e.g., the unsigned editorial in *Interpretation* 42 (1988), 3–4; in these two pages some form of the word 'advocacy' appears no fewer than seven times to describe feminism and its proponents, but not once to characterize its critics. Yet they too advocate.

26. Cf. Judith Plaskow, 'Christian Feminism and Anti-Judaism', *Cross Currents* 28 (1978), 306–9. For a sampling of diversity within Jewish feminism, see 'Feminist Consciousness Today, Roundtable: The Women's Movement', *Tikkun* 2 (1987), 40–46. See Plaskow, *Standing Again at Sinai: Judaism from a Feminist Perspective*, New York: Harper & Row 1990 and Edinburgh: T.&T. Clark 1991. Cf. most recently papers delivered at the third conference of the European Society of Women for Theological Research. Collected under the general heading 'Feminist Anti-Judaism', they were published in the *Journal of Feminist Studies in Religion* 7 (1991), 95–133.

27. See Letty M. Russell, et al. (eds), *Inheriting our Mothers' Gardens: Feminist Theology in Third World Perspective*, Philadelphia: Westminster Press 1978. With increasing unease I keep the terms First and Third Worlds. Though they belong to common parlance, they may suggest elitism, condescension, and inaccuracy. The last becomes particularly true with the break-up of the so-called Second World.

28. The term 'womanist' derives from Alice Walker, *In Search of our Mothers' Gardens: Womanist Prose*, San Diego: Harcourt Brace Jovanovich 1983, esp. xi–xii. Cf. Paula Giddings, *When and Where I Enter: The Impact of Black Women on Race and Sex in America*, New York: William Morrow 1984.

29. Cf. Naomi R. Goldenberg, *Changing of the Gods: Feminism and the End of Traditional Religions*, Boston: Beacon Press 1979, esp. 10–25.

30. Cf., e.g., Merlin Stone, *When God Was a Woman*, New York: The Dial Press 1976.

31. For current discussion, see above note 26.
32. Cf., e.g., the interaction of critical, rabbinical, and feminist views in Kathryn Pfisterer Darr, *Far More Precious than Jewels: Perspectives on Biblical Women*, Louisville, KY: Westminster/John Knox Press 1991.
33. Collections exemplifying various responses include *The Bible and Feminist Hermeneutics, Semeia* 28, ed. Mary Ann Tolbert, Chico, CA: Scholars Press 1983; *Feminist Perspectives on Biblical Scholarship*, ed. Adela Yarbro Collins, Chico, CA: Scholars Press 1985; *Feminist Interpretation of the Bible*, ed. Letty M. Russell, Philadelphia: Westminster Press and Oxford: Blackwell 1985; *Reasoning with the Foxes: Female Wit in a World of Male Power, Semeia* 42, ed. J. Cheryl Exum and Johanna W.H. Bos, Atlanta, GA: Scholars Press 1988; *Ad Feminam, Union Seminary Quarterly Review* 43, ed. Alice Bach (1989), passim; *Gender and Difference in Ancient Israel*, ed. Peggy L. Day, Minneapolis: Fortress 1989, a volume that identifies itself as 'primarily non-theological' (xiii).
34. Phyllis Bird, ' "To Play the Harlot": An Inquiry into an Old Testament Metaphor', *Gender and Difference in Ancient Israel*, 75–94; id., 'The Place of Women in the Israelite Cultus', *Ancient Israelite Religion*, ed. Patrick D. Miller, Jr, Paul D. Hanson, S. Dean McBride, Philadelphia: Fortress Press, 1987, 397–419; id., 'Images of Women in the Old Testament', *Religion and Sexism*, ed. Rosemary Radford Ruether, New York: Simon and Schuster 1974, 41–88.
35. Jo Ann Hackett, 'Women's Studies and the Hebrew Bible', *The Future of Biblical Studies*, ed. Richard Elliott Friedmann and H.G.M. Williamson, Atlanta, GA: Scholars Press 1987, 141–164. Cf. id., 'Rehabilitating Hagar: Fragments of an Epic Pattern', *Gender and Difference in Ancient Israel*, 12–27.
36. Carol Meyers, *Discovering Eve: Ancient Israelite Women in Context*, New York: Oxford University Press 1988; cf. esp. 23, 187.
37. J. Cheryl Exum, ' "You Shall Let Every Daughter Live": A Study of Exodus 1:8–2:10', *The Bible and Feminist Hermeneutics, Semeia* 28, ed. Mary Ann Tolbert, Chico, CA: Scholars Press 1983, 63–82. Id., ' "Mother in Israel": A Familiar Figure Reconsidered', *Feminist Interpretation of the Bible*, ed. Letty M. Russell, Philadelphia: Westminster Press and Oxford: Blackwell 1985, 73–85. In her more recent work, Exum adopts a harsher view toward the text itself, with ample use of the adjective 'phallocentric'; see, e.g., 'Murder They Wrote: Ideology and the Manipulation of Female Presence in Biblical Narrative', *Ad Feminam*, 19–39.
38. Toni Craven, 'Tradition and Convention in the Book of Judith', *The Bible and Feminist Hermeneutics, Semeia* 28, ed. Mary Ann Tolbert, Chico, CA: Scholars Press 1983, 49–61. See also id., 'Women Who Lied

for the Faith', *Justice and the Holy*, ed. Douglas A. Knight and Peter J. Paris, Atlanta, GA: Scholars Press 1989.

39. Claudia V. Camp, *Wisdom and the Feminine in the Book of Proverbs*, Sheffield: Almond, JSOT Press 1985; also id., 'Wise and Strange: An Interpretation of the Female Imagery in Proverbs in Light of Trickster Mythology', *Reasoning With the Foxes, Semeia* 42, 14–36.

40. Tikva Frymer-Kensky, 'The Strange Case of the Suspected Sotah (Numbers V 11–31)', *Vetus Testamentum* 34 (1984), 11–26.

41. Tikva Frymer-Kensky, 'Law and Philosophy: The Case of Sex in the Bible', *Thinking Biblical Law, Semeia* 45, ed. Dale Patrick, Atlanta, GA: Scholars Press 1989, 89–102. The quotation comes from p. 99.

42. Tikva Frymer-Kensky, *In the Wake of the Goddesses: Women, Culture, and the Biblical Transformation of Pagan Myth*, New York: The Free Press 1992.

43. Athalya Brenner, *The Israelite Women*, Sheffield: JSOT Press 1985.

44. Renita J. Weems, *Just a Sister Away*, ix. The combination proposed gives more weight to storytelling than to biblical criticism. Cf. also id., 'Gomer: Victim of Violence or Victim of Metaphor', *Interpretation for Liberation, Semeia* 47, 87–104.

45. Alice L. Laffey, *An Introduction to the Old Testament: A Feminist Perspective*, Philadelphia: Fortress Press 1988 (= *Wives, Harlots and Concubines: The Old Testament in Feminist Perspective*, London: SPCK 1990). Regrettably, numerous factual errors mar this book.

46. See most recently *The Women's Bible Commentary*, ed. Carol A. Newsom and Sharon H. Ringe, Philadelphia: Westminister Press and London: SPCK 1992, 'the first comprehensive attempt to gather some of the fruits of feminist biblical scholarship on each book of the Bible in order to share it with the larger community of women who read the Bible.'

47. See Elisabeth Schüssler Fiorenza, 'The Ethics of Biblical Interpretation: Decentering Biblical Scholarship', *Journal of Biblical Literature* (1988), 3–17.

48. This discussion draws heavily upon Phyllis Trible, 'A Love Story Gone Awry', *God and the Rhetoric of Sexuality*, Philadelphia: Fortress Press 1978 and London: SCM Press 1992, 72–143.

49. Cf. Ex. 18.4; Deut. 33.7, 26, 29; Ps. 121.2; 124.8; 146.5.

50. Eichrodt, *Theology of the Old Testament I*, 56–58 and passim: ibid., vol. II, passim; von Rad, *Old Testament Theology*, I, 7f., 170f., 394f.; ibid., II, passim.

51. Terrien, *The Elusive Presence*, 63–105.

52. This discussion incorporates two earlier studies: Phyllis Trible, 'Hagar: The Desolation of Rejection', *Texts of Terror*, Philadelphia: Fortress Press 1984 and London: SCM Press 1992, 9–35; id., 'Genesis 22: The Sacrifice of Sarah', '*Not In Heaven*', ed. Jason P. Rosenblatt and Joseph

C. Sitterson, Jr, Bloomington, IN: Indiana University Press 1991, 170–191.

53. Contra Phyllis Bird, ' "Male and Female He Created Them": Gen 1:27b in the Context of the Priestly Account of Creation', *Harvard Theological Review* 74 (1981), 129–159, a study that assigns the text but a single meaning and that a narrow one (procreation). Such restriction the text imposes neither upon itself nor upon the reader.

54. See Z. Meshel and Carol Meyers, 'The Name of God in the Wilderness of Zin', *Biblical Archaeology* 39 (1976), 11–17; William G. Dever, 'Consort of Yahweh? New Evidence from Kuntillet 'Ajrud', *Bulletin of the American School of Oriental Research* 255 (1984), 21–37; John Day, 'Asherah in the Hebrew Bible and Northwest Semitic Literature', *Journal of Biblical Literature* 105 (1986), 385–408; Judith M. Hadly, 'Some Drawings and Inscriptions on Two Pithoi from Kuntillet 'Ajrud', *Vetus Testamentum* 37 (1987), 180–213; Baruch Margalit, 'The Meaning and Significance of Asherah', *Vetus Testamentum* 40 (1990), 264–297 with bibliography.

55. Cf. Patrick D. Miller, 'Israelite Religion', *The Hebrew Bible and Its Modern Interpreters*, ed. Douglas A. Knight and Gene M. Tucker, Philadelphia: Fortress Press 1985, 201–237; Mark S. Smith, *The Early History of God*, San Francisco: Harper & Row 1990, passim.

56. See Trible, *God and the Rhetoric of Sexuality*, 31–71; cf. Smith, *The Early History of God*, 97–103.

57. For patriarchal interpretations, see, e.g., Hans Walter Wolff, *Hosea, Hermeneia*, Philadelphia: Fortress Press 1974, 197–203; James Luther Mays, *Hosea*, Philadelphia: Westminster Press 1969, 150–159. Francis I. Andersen and David Noel Freedman avoid the issue by using the gender-neutral term *parent, Hosea*, The Anchor Bible, Doubleday 1980, 574–583. While acknowledging the presence of maternal imagery, Terrien nevertheless denigrates the female in his interpretation by suggesting that Hosea assumed maternal duties neglected by the wayward Gomer (*Till the Heart Sings*, 56). Severe textual problems throughout this passage render the translation and interpretation difficult.

58. Cf. the RSV which reads, 'for I am God and not man'.

59. Cf. Erhard S. Gerstenberger, *Jahwe – ein patriarchaler Gott? Traditionelles Gottesbild und feministische Theologie*, Stuttgart: W. Kohlhammer 1988.

60. See Letty M. Russell, *Household of Freedom: Authority in Feminist Theology*, Philadelphia: Westminster Press 1987; Claudia V. Camp, 'Female Voice, Written Word: Women and Authority in Hebrew Scripture', *Embodied Love* ed. Paula M. Cooey, Sharon A. Farmer, Mary Ellen Ross, San Francisco: Harper & Row 1987, 97–113; Sharon H. Ringe, 'When Women Interpret the Bible', *The Women's Bible Commentary*, 1–9.

3

Liberating the Reader: A Theological-Exegetical Study of the Parable of the Sheep and the Goats (Matt. 25.31–46)

Francis Watson

It is a well-known fact that goods manufactured in Third World countries are often excluded from Western markets by a system of trade restrictions designed to protect local industries. Is it possible that an analogous system is operative in the field of intellectual production? The theology of liberation, a Third World product, has for over two decades been attempting to interpret the biblical texts in a manner which is responsive both to modern theological debate and to certain of the elementary sociopolitical realities of our world. While some First World theologians have listened to what is being said, the theology of liberation has made only a limited impact in the marketplace of contemporary biblical studies.

Here, a system of restrictions protects a mode of intellectual production which is often both inefficient and expensive. Many producers seem content merely to recycle old ideas and old problems, offering ever more precise and precarious answers to questions whose significance for interpretation is quite wrongly regarded as self-evident. Fortunately, biblical scholars are not condemned to this treadmill, for in the more innovative sectors a range of new paradigms is being developed; in the case of literary, feminist and sociohistorical perspectives, for example, the work already produced indicates that these paradigms are capable of sustaining a broadly-based, communal interpretative practice. In the case of the theology of liberation, however, no such communal practice has yet established itself in a First World setting. Individual biblical scholars have attempted to respond to the concerns of liberation theology, and some valuable and provocative work has been produced;[1] and yet this work so far remains at the level of suggestive individual contributions, and there is little sign of the convergence of assumptions and procedures necessary for the development of a new paradigm.

How are we to explain the non-occurrence of any serious, sustained encounter between First World biblical studies and Third World liberation theology? There are factors on both sides of the divide which readily account for this non-event.

The products of liberation theology are in general not oriented towards First World biblical studies; they do not meet, or attempt to meet, the criteria for participation in the conversation. We do not find many commentaries on individual books written from this perspective, nor do we encounter many monographs or articles devoted to more specific interpretative issues. Theologies of liberation characteristically issue from contexts where the idea of a relatively autonomous biblical studies which distances itself from the broader theological endeavour is still alien. In such a context, biblical interpretation will occur at a relatively high level of generality: broad appeals to, for example, Jesus' proclamation of the kingdom of God will be more common than a concern with the exegetical intricacies which, for First World scholars, surround this particular issue. Historical-critical study of the Bible has had a major impact on theologies of liberation, and Western biblical scholars are frequently cited; yet the emphasis has been upon the theological appropriation of their work rather than on developing a dialogue with them on their own terms. Most of the major figures of Latin American liberation theology – Gutiérrez, Leonardo and Clodovis Boff, Sobrino and Segundo, for example – are primarily theologians rather than biblical scholars.[2]

Sometimes one does encounter the beginnings of a critique of the procedures and priorities of First World biblical studies. Carlos Mesters, for example, asserts that 'exegesis, for lack of contact with life, is in danger of ... getting lost in the meanderings of its own speculations, turning the exegete into a technocrat of the Bible'.[3] Yet the function of such hermeneutical claims is not primarily to reform the practice of First World exegesis but to challenge its prestige and question its adequacy within the Latin American context. In terms of biblical interpretation, the fundamental datum of that context is the popular sociopolitical reading of the Bible within the 'base communities', and the sophisticated hermeneutical reflection of, say, Clodovis Boff takes this as its starting-point and ignores the normal concerns of European and North American exegesis.[4] Few Western exegetes have any experience at all of popular sociopolitical reading of the Bible from the standpoint of the poor and oppressed. Their only non-academic point of reference is typically a pietistic, apolitical Bible-reading stemming from the socially and economically secure middle classes to which they themselves also belong. It is easy to conclude from this that the two contexts are so different that communication and interaction are hardly worth attempting – a view which is assumed, *de facto*, by most First World biblical scholars. Whether one claims that the European and North American exegetical tradition is superior to the Latin American one, or, with a show of modesty, that the two traditions and their contexts are simply 'different', the outcome is the same either way: the First World continues to define itself as the centre while the Third World is assigned to the periphery.[5] It is worth exploring further the means by which this construction is maintained.

The pietistic tradition of private, 'devotional' Bible-reading, to which I have just referred, faithfully reproduces the characteristic First World privatization of religion which dissociates it from the public, political sphere. The public ideological role that religion once exercised has to a large extent been assumed by other agencies (education and the media, for example), and the potential for social conflict that religion possesses as a public entity is contained by assigning religious commitment to the sphere of free personal choice. 'Tolerance' is promoted as a way of enforcing the narrow limits thereby established. Naturally this situation is neither unambiguous nor unproblematic; various modes of resistance to it can be detected, and many vestiges of a different social arrangement still persist. Yet as a broad generalization it is probably true to say that in most First World contexts individuals are socialized into a view which equates religion with the personal and the private and which militates against its significant public functioning. In another sense, indeed, religion continues to exercise a public ideological role precisely in this privatized form: for the exaltation of the private sphere at the expense of the public one is a highly political act which makes possible a range of evasions and concealments of the more brutal realities of the public sphere. Privatized religion is by no means as apolitical as it claims. Nevertheless, it has been promoted so successfully that the separation of 'religion' and 'politics' has come to seem self-evident, a necessary truth of reason.

Biblical scholars, being ordinary and unremarkable members of society, also participate in this socialization process. They believe, indeed, that what they still sometimes call the 'objective' study of the Bible is of public significance, but only in so far as this activity is defined in largely secular terms. The effect of this secularizing or desacralizing of the Bible is further to reinforce the privatization of religious commitment. Biblical scholarship understands itself as public discourse, admittedly of a very specialized kind, and must therefore necessarily exclude religious commitment from its frame of reference; not because the existential significance of such a commitment is denied but because the dominant public discourse refuses to hold an opinion on this topic, speaking only of the freedom and sanctity of personal choice and the duty of tolerance. The two apparently contradictory traditions of 'devotional reading' and 'critical study' of the Bible turn out to occupy two sides of the same ideological schema: both activities perpetuate the construction of religious commitment as private, personal, a matter of conviction and faith, ultimately incommunicable by normal rational means. There is little difference in this respect between the naive reading in which the Bible is simply and straightforwardly 'the Word of God' and the refined or attenuated mysticism of the postcritical intellectual – except perhaps that the privatizing of religious commitment has been taken still further in the second case than in the first.

The theology of liberation might well be understood, at least within a First World context, as the systematic, uncompromising exposure and rejection of this privatizing of religious commitment.[6] It is, precisely, a *theology*, a discourse about the origin and destiny of existence conceived as a structured whole. The dualistic demarcation of the authentic subjective sphere from the inauthentic objective one is unmasked as an ideological construct, and the deity manifested only in the inwardness of the former is rejected as an idol. An anti-dualistic conception of God is inseparable from an anti-dualistic conception of social existence which, if it is to fulfil its critical role, must bring to light the rationale of the dualistic view as a mode of *concealment*. What has society got to hide that it should distort the truth about itself in this way, pretending that at its deepest level human being is not social and relational but monadic? What is hidden is the extent to which social relations between humans are relations of oppression, and the intractability of this situation is to be found not only in the fact of the injustice itself but also in its concealment beneath a veneer of normality. Institutionalized injustice is at least as destructive in its effects as exceptional, blatant, visible acts of injustice and violence, but its peculiar characteristic is to efface itself, to deny its own existence, to represent itself as normality, necessity and realism. The illusion is especially effective among the beneficiaries of the status quo, but even the oppressed may be persuaded to internalize to some degree the dominant construction of reality and thus to fulfil the roles allotted to them by the ruling class.

The theology of liberation is, in part, an attempt to reflect upon the biblical texts in the light of this situation of institutionalized oppression. Although it stems from a location considerably closer to the victims of this oppression than does most First World theology, it does not make the mistake of focussing too exclusively on the immediate symptoms of oppression – for example, the flagrant and appalling abuse of human rights to which the ruling elites of some Latin American countries habitually resort in order to shore up their hold on power.[7] If liberation theology were simply a protest against human rights abuses, it would be easy to regard it as determined by a context quite different from our own within the democracies of the First World. In its concern with institutionalized, structural oppression, however, liberation theology attempts to see oppression as a global phenomenon in which we too are implicated, through our participation in a political and economic order in which a minority prospers at the expense of the majority. The claim that liberation theology has nothing to do with us because our situation is different overlooks precisely the material factors which make our privileged situation possible in the first place.

First World exegetes are therefore not excluded from the task of reflection on the biblical texts in the light of a situation of institutionalized oppression, since that situation is global. Yet we should be under no illusions about the strict limitations within which such a project would operate. Sociopolitical reading of the Bible in San Salvador may have been sufficiently effective to bring the death squads into the slums, the cathedral and the university; but if First World theologians and exegetes are spared such horrors, they also seem condemned to ineffectiveness beyond the very limited sphere of those who take an interest in their labours. A reading of the Book of Amos, or of the Epistle of James, is not likely to do much to alter the inequities and iniquities of the Third World debt crisis. A mode of interpretation that was both theologically and politically responsible might, however, be of some significance within the Christian community. In this context, the secularizing ideology which treats the biblical texts as mere historical artefacts can never be the whole truth about those texts; and, if there is anything at all in their claim to offer good news to the poor, popular tendencies to spiritualize and privatize the biblical message need not have the last word either. It would not be much, but it would at least be something, to share in the development of a paradigm for biblical interpretation which sought to integrate the project of human solidarity more securely within Christian identity and praxis.

In developing such a paradigm, it is important to make use of all the resources that our contemporary interpretative situation offers us. The theology of liberation has in the past been able to make good use of some of the insights of the historical-critical perspective, and there is no justification for calls to abandon this perspective altogether. The work of Norman Gottwald indicates the fruitfulness of historical method for a politically-aware interpretative practice.[8] At the same time, it is becoming increasingly obvious that the dominance of this perspective has unnecessarily constricted the range of our interpretative options, and an ability to appropriate the insights of perspectives stemming from resistance to the dominant paradigm is therefore also required: feminist and narrative criticism would be obvious examples, together with the explorations of contemporary hermeneutics and literary theory into the role of the reader in the production of meaning. Finally, if liberation theology is indeed a 'theology', and if Christian praxis is one of its points of reference, then exegesis from within this perspective must be oriented towards relevant theological issues and should abandon the false modesty which insists that matters of theology are outside the competence of biblical scholarship. What I envisage, in other words, is an exegetical practice able to make eclectic though critical use of a variety of interpretative strategies, deriving its coherence not from any methodological purity but from its orientation towards the political-theological task.

The reading that follows of Jesus' parable of the sheep and the goats (Matt. 25.31–46) is a preliminary attempt at an interpretative practice of the kind I have just outlined.

1. What is said and what is meant

In his *Theology of Liberation*,[9] Gustavo Gutiérrez appeals to Matt. 25.31–46 in developing Congar's theme of 'the sacrament of the neighbour'. Appropriating and extending a biblical image, Gutiérrez represents the human person as the 'temple of God', and this means that communion with God requires human mediation: 'It is not enough to say that love of God is inseparable from the love of one's neighbour. It must be added that love for God is unavoidably expressed *through* love of one's neighbour' (114–15). Indeed, in the parable love of the neighbour is given a certain priority over love for God, for it is only subsequently, at the judgment, that the full theological meaning of the actions of the righteous on behalf of the needy is disclosed. This text does not suggest that love for the neighbour must be motivated by a prior, explicit love for God or Christ, a situation that might in fact compromise the reality or integrity of love for the neighbour. 'The neighbour is not an occasion, an instrument, for becoming closer to God. We are dealing with a real love of persons for their own sake and not "for the love of God," as the well-meant but ambiguous and ill-used cliché would have it – ambiguous and ill-used because many seem to interpret it in a sense which forgets that the love for God is expressed in a true love for persons themselves' (116). This love 'leads us far beyond the individualistic language of the I-Thou relationship', for the term 'neighbour' refers 'to a person considered in the fabric of social relationships, to a person situated in economic, social, cultural, and racial coordinates' (116).

As Gutiérrez also notes, however, 'exegetes are alarmed by the way that many theologians use this text' (112), and this situation – so typical of the tension between historical-critical and theological readings of a text – merits hermeneutical reflection. The problem arises from v. 40 ('Truly I say to you, as you did it to one of the least of these my brothers, you did it to me'). Over against the assumption that this refers universally to all the poor and oppressed, many exegetes wish to adopt a drastically restricted reading in which 'my

63

brothers' refers to the disciples and/or the Christian community.[10] From within the historical-critical paradigm, this conclusion is moderately plausible, although not compelling; and, in making the treatment of the Christian community the criterion of judgment, the outcome is that this text becomes theologically worthless.[11] I shall set out a conventional case for this restricted reading which will be followed by consideration of the hermeneutical issues it raises.

The first point in favour of the restrictive view is the Matthean usage elsewhere of the theme of Christ's 'brothers'. In Matt. 12.49, it is the disciples (rather than the crowds) who are addressed as 'my mother and my brothers', and this is extended in the following verse to include the Christian community: 'Whoever does the will of my Father in heaven is my brother, and sister, and mother.' In 28.10, the risen Jesus instructs the women to 'go and tell my brothers to go to Galilee'. To these instances we might also add the more general use of the term 'brother' to refer to a member of the Christian community in, for example, 18.15 ('If your brother sins against you ...') and 23.8 ('you are all brothers'). All this suggests that in 25.40 the criterion at the judgment is treatment of Christians rather than the poor and oppressed in general.[12]

Second, the reference to various forms of suffering may suggest – still more restrictively – that it is itinerant preachers who are specifically referred to: the catalogue of sufferings – hunger, thirst, homelessness, nakedness, sickness, imprisonment – recalls Pauline statements such as Rom. 8.35 (hunger, nakedness), I Cor. 4.11 (hunger, thirst, nakedness and homelessness), II Cor. 11.23–27 (imprisonment, hunger, thirst, nakedness) and Gal.4.13–14 (sickness).[13] In relieving the suffering of his missionaries, people are serving Christ himself: 'He who receives you receives me ... And whoever gives to one of these little ones even a cup of cold water *because he is a disciple*, truly, I say to you, he shall not lose his reward' (Matt. 10.40,42). 'I was thirsty and you gave me a drink' (Matt. 25.35): that is, when the addressee gave a cup of cold water to a disciple.

Third, the presence of 'my brothers' alongside the enthroned Christ suggests a reference to the twelve disciples: 'When the Son of man shall sit on his glorious throne, you who have followed me will also sit on twelve thrones, judging the twelve tribes of Israel' (Matt. 19.28). Admittedly in 25.32 it is *panta ta ethnē* rather that the tribes of Israel who are being judged, but the parallel is still close enough to suggest a reference to the twelve disciples in 25.40. Their relationship with the *ethnē* is confirmed by their commission to 'make disciples of all nations' (28.19).

These considerations leave some ambiguity about whether the 'brothers' of 25.40 are Christians in general or itinerant missionaries;[14] but the significant point here is that they seem to exclude the universalizing reading necessary for Gutiérrez's theological reflections. Once again, the encounter between theology and exegesis betrays the familiar pattern described by Heikki Räisänen: 'While it is very hard to discover how one should go about using the Bible positively in theology, if one is not simply to fall back on pre-critical modes, it is surely possible to point out cases of overly strained application or downright misuse of the documents. At the very least, exegesis can function as the "historical conscience" of theology.'[15] In its self-appointed role as historical conscience, exegesis informs theology that the real meaning of the parable of the sheep and the goats is more or less the opposite of what it had supposed: the allegedly universal criterion turns out to be thoroughly particularist.

Increased hermeneutical awareness may help us to avoid this dispiriting conclusion. In the conventional historical-critical argument I outlined, interpretation was determined by a complex of (mainly Matthean) passages external to the one under discussion. No one, reading Matt. 25.31–46 in isolation, would suppose that its subject is the treatment of Christian evangelists. Within this text, the 'brothers' are characterized only as hungry, thirsty, homeless, naked, sick and imprisoned; nothing is said about their either making disciples (cf. 28.19) or being disciples (cf. 19.28). Yet, in the conventional exegetical procedure, the apparent literal sense of this text has to be subordinated to other texts scattered throughout the Gospel, a procedure justified by appeal to authorial intention understood as a means of imposing relative unity on apparently heterogeneous material. What appears to be the literal sense of the parable is sacrificed for the sake of the unity of the whole as it is imagined to have existed in its author's mind. 'Matthew' may indeed have understood the parable in the restricted sense, but his intention remains a hypothetical entity insufficiently externalized in the actual wording of the text as it stands. In other words, we may appeal to the letter of the text against the author who, absented from his text in the very act of writing, can only be speculatively reunited with his text by an allegorical or spiritualizing reading which seeks to penetrate the letter of the text in pursuit of the more fundamental entity that it is said to conceal: here, an imperfectly expressed authorial intention to which the entire text of the Gospel of Matthew is to be subordinated. But what if the author refuses to play this game? What if, as we tell him what he should have said to make his meaning clearer, he simply refers us back to the text with the words, 'What I have written, I have written'? The hermeneutical principle of the absence of the author from the text is a useful way of countering the reductionist tendency to confine textual meaning to the reconstructed circumstances of origin.

The text as it stands is clearly open to the kind of reading represented by Gutiérrez. There is nothing in its wording, its literal sense, that forbids such a reading, and much that encourages it. The opposing reading is also a possible reading: the hypothesis of the unifying authorial intention cannot be excluded, and it may indeed lead to insight into the world of the Matthean community.[16] In so far as it attempts to exclude the theological reading, however, by representing itself as what the text 'really' means, it oversteps the limits of its own competence. It also exposes itself to criticism of its ideological stance: for its effect is to reinforce the privatizing of religious commitment and the subjection of religion to a secularizing discourse within the public sphere. A religious commitment – the expression of love for God only by way of love for the neighbour – initially claims a certain basis for itself in the relatively public form of a communally authoritative text. This basis is then removed by a secularizing exegesis, and the effect is to reduce that commitment to a private, personal opinion with no conceivable basis in the now secularized public world. This apparently self-evident outcome in fact derives its force from the prior decision of certain societies to confine religion to the narrow sphere of private preference. Since the theology of liberation opposes this decision, an exegesis that assumes it is simply begging the question.

Gutiérrez's reading reflects in general terms on what he takes to be the central theme of the Matthean passage; but it is not, strictly speaking, an exegesis of this passage. The question this raises is whether it is possible to practise the theological and the exegetical tasks simultaneously. Having raised some of the hermeneutical issues, I hope to demonstrate the possibility of a fruitful interaction between theology and exegesis in what follows.

2. *The anonymous Christ*

It may be desirable for a theologically-oriented exegesis to begin by reflecting upon the limitations of the passage in question: partly in furtherance of its own proper task, and partly in opposition to the assumption that a theological appropriation of a text must assume a perfect coincidence between itself and the 'real meaning' of the text. There are at least two points where one must judge this particular Matthean text theologically inadequate.

First, as in so much of the Bible, its language is naively androcentric. Its central figure is described by the narrator as 'the Son of man' (v. 31) and 'the King' (vv. 34, 40), and is also compared to a 'shepherd' (v. 32). He is addressed by those on his right and on his left as 'Lord' (vv. 37, 44). He comes as the emissary of his 'Father', and the criterion by which he judges is the treatment of his 'brothers'. The term 'brother' does not naturally include 'sister', any more than 'son' includes 'daughter' or 'father' includes 'mother': thus the one who does the will of the heavenly Father is Jesus' brother *or sister* (Matt. 12.50), and his literal sisters are differentiated from his brothers – although, since they are regarded as less important, their names are not given (13.55–56). Yet it is one of the curious illusions of the androcentric outlook that exclusively male terminology can be used in a universal sense. 'You are all brothers', says Jesus to the disciples (23.8), denying by his exclusive use of this term the egalitarianism which it is the purpose of the whole passage to promote. And how are we to respond to the fact that the ultimate judge and criterion of all humanity is portrayed here and everywhere in the New Testament as a male figure? Are the wrongs done to women done 'to him'? Does he know anything of these specific gender-related wrongs? Such questions are unanswerable from within the limits of this particular text, but the fact that they arise here once again exposes the curiously persistent idea of the pristine perfection of the canonical texts as a myth.

Secondly, the parable is compatible with an individualizing, personalistic view of 'charity' which abstracts both giver and receiver from the social context which in fact assigns them their respective roles.[17] In such a construction, wealth and poverty are naturalized, and there is no recognition of the interdependence of wealth and poverty, the ways in which the enrichment of the few is achieved at the expense of the impoverishment of the many. Feeding the hungry is often an absolute imperative, but this very act may be converted to ideological use in reinforcing the perception of the giver's excess and the receiver's privation as a 'natural' state of affairs, about which no further questions can or should be asked. What the poor need from the rich is not so much charity as justice, and a reading of the parable that failed to acknowledge this would be placing itself at the disposal of ideologies that strive to conceal this objective situation. It is not the case that the link between deprivation and structural injustice is a purely modern perception, for it is explicit in the prophets and implicit in the gospels' condemnations of the rich.[18]

Awareness of such limitations will exclude all idealizing of the biblical text, all claims that one must submit one's critical faculties beneath the imperious demands of a semi-divinized book. However, critical awareness may be employed in the opening up of a text's constructive possibilities as well as in exposing its potentially negative dimensions. What kind of contemporary theological reflection does this particular text open up?

In the parable, the events of parousia and judgment or separation are depicted in summary fashion: the Son of man returns and judgment occurs, in accordance with the traditional schema (vv. 31–33). Interest is focussed not on these events in themselves but on the rationale that underlies the act of separation (vv. 34–46).[19] The shepherd who separates sheep and goats does so on the basis of simple external criteria, but it is not clear what criteria are to be employed in the division of 'all the nations'. When the criteria are finally announced, they surprise both righteous and unrighteous alike. A backward reference is made to certain acts, performed in the one case, neglected in the other. The king himself was the beneficiary of those acts, and it was he who suffered when they were neglected. That is to say, the august, glorious figure on the throne has previously been present to all the peoples of the world in a quite different way: as hungry, thirsty, homeless, naked, sick and imprisoned, as a victim, in other words, of the typical social evils to which most humans have always been exposed. This king was once present in the most unkingly of forms, the diametrical opposite of his present enthroned majesty. Some gave him the assistance he needed while others refused it, and it is their treatment of him which now determines whether they enter the kingdom prepared for them from the foundation of the world or depart into the eternal fire prepared for the devil and his angels.

The narrative is set in the future, as is indicated by the future tenses of the verbs employed by the narrator. Yet, in posing the question of the rationale for the act of separation, the attention of both groups is directed to what for them is past although for the reader it is present: the unlikely presence of the king as the victim to whom all people on earth either render assistance or culpably fail to do so. The reader is directed back to his or her present by way of this detour into the future. The surprised questions ('Lord, when did we see thee ...?') thus coincide with the reader's own question as to where in the present the king is to be found fulfilling his unexpected role as the victim in desperate need of assistance. For the reader, that is to say, statements about the past ('I was hungry and you gave me food') have a certain imperative force for the present; the Son of man is in our midst, he is hungry and must be fed. But where is he to be found, that we may give him the assistance he needs? The answer takes the form of another epiphany. All peoples of the world are gathered before the king, everyone is apparently accounted for, and yet a third group in addition to the righteous and the unrighteous is suddenly brought into focus as the key to the mystery of the king's former presence as victim: a group indicated with a gesture of the hand as 'these my brothers' or simply as 'these'. Even within this group, a certain discrimination takes place, for the king points in particular to '*the least* of these (my brothers)', although with the implication that what is true of them is true also of the others. Who are they? All we know is that they are victims of deprivation and injustice and that they are universally present to be either assisted or neglected by all peoples of the world, at every time and in every place. Their universality indicates that they are, quite simply, all victims of deprivation and injustice; no other distinguishing characteristic is given, and no other is needed. The king's solidarity with the op-pressed is so complete that he can speak of himself as suffering their oppression, and yet the effect of the epiphany of his brothers and sisters is to divert the attention that has so far been focussed on his majestic form on to them. They are the solution to the riddle the king has propounded; they are the key to the mystery of the judgment; indeed, in that the judgment manifests the meaning of the world, they are the key to the mystery of the world itself. The treatment received by the poor lies at the heart of the riddle of the world. Their own epiphany as the solution to the King's riddle discloses the ultimate foundations of the world in a way that even his own seemingly more impressive epiphany does not. His own significance is now to be found not in the personal power and glory which enable him to control the destiny of humans and angels but in his un-qualified solidarity with the poor. Thus, their epiphany is the fulfilment of his own: his revelation in glory is at the same time his revelation as the one who suffers with the oppressed and in their sufferings. His unqualified identification with the oppressed is the meaning of his glory.

What does all this mean for the Matthean reader? Such a figure is, of course, an interpretative construct. The hypothesis of the implied reader, encoded within the text, must be supplemented by recogni-tion of the interpretative freedom integral to any real act of reading: the freedom, for example, to actualize certain potential connections and not others, the freedom to emphasize and de-emphasize in accordance with one's own criteria of relevance.[20] The 'Matthean reader' whom I shall postulate is a semi-fictional character who must nevertheless be made plausible within the constraints of the text.

The epiphany of the Son of man here takes the form of a text and is therefore directed primarily towards the reader. What is it that this epiphany discloses to the reader? The coming of the Son of man in his glory is already a well-known topic, and from the reader's stand-point the recurrence of this topic here is not in itself disclosive of anything new. Thus the passage opens with the phrase, '*When* the Son of man comes in his glory', referring to that which is already familiar. As we have seen, however, the reader shares the perplexity of both of the separated groups in the parable. Yet for sheep and goats alike, the king's solution to his own riddle is the final, eschatological disclosure. No further questions are conceivable: the revelation of the meaning of the world establishes the ultimate destiny of the two groups as eternal life or eternal punishment, and there is nothing more to be said. The reader, on the other hand, is still on the way and has not yet reached that place of disclosure. The textual anticipation of that final disclosure therefore raises many questions and leaves much still to be said, more especially because it runs counter to the expectations generated by the narrative up to this point. The Matthean implied reader not only reads but also par-ticipates in the communal life of the *ekklesia*; the instructions about the constitution of that communal life in Matt. 18 are intended to be recognizable in current communal practice. As a member of the *ekklesia*, the reader echoes Simon Peter's confession ('You are the

Christ, the Son of the living God'), upon which the church is built, and shares in the assurance that this acknowledgment derives not from flesh and blood but from the will of the heavenly Father (16.16-18). An actual reader who reads the Gospel of Matthew outside this context of community and confession is obviously thinkable, but he or she will bear no relation to the implied reader projected in the text itself. Granted this communal, confessional setting, the impact of the anticipatory disclosure of the end in Matt. 25.31-46 is catastrophic, appearing to overturn the image of the Son of man thus far constructed and undermining the identity constituted by association with this figure; for the scandalous message of this text is that the distinction between righteous and unrighteous is unrelated to the distinction between church and world, and that the final criterion will be the Christ secretly present among the oppressed rather than the Christ openly acknowledged within the community.[21] The righteous are not righteous because they acknowledged Christ – there is no indication of any such failure. Righteousness springs from an encounter with the anonymous Christ of which one is entirely unaware, and this can take place only in the service of the oppressed. Unrighteousness derives from the neglect of this service, and this is entirely compatible with a confession of Christ that is both heartfelt and orthodox. The parable of the sheep and the goats asserts both the secret solidarity of the Son of man with the oppressed and the possibility that his true servants are those who know nothing of him but only seek to serve their oppressed neighbour.[22] The heathen may act not so much as 'anonymous Christians' but as servants of the anonymous Christ.

The parable that discloses all this, critically situated at the junction between Jesus' ministry and the passion narrative, threatens to subvert the text to which it belongs by rendering it superfluous. The Gospel of Matthew asserts its own absolute indispensability at the outset, when the angel announces the birth of one who 'will save his people from their sins' (1.21); and during the course of the gospel narrative this announcement gradually assumes concrete form. And yet the whole of this rich, manifold depiction, projecting an entire world within which one may live and move and have one's being, is threatened with redundancy when the service of the oppressed is made the sole criterion of the final disclosure, and when this service is identified as the locus for the saving encounter with a Christ who remains hidden in it. Naturally the church should perform works of mercy to the oppressed inside and outside its own communal boundaries, and in so far as it does so its members will be found among the sheep rather than the goats. But if the works of justice and mercy are regarded as the sole criterion, then the communal and confessional context out of which they proceed is irrelevant. Even the worshippers of idols, who constitute the overwhelming majority in the group designated as *panta ta ethnē* (25.32), may feed the hungry and visit the prisoners; and in so far as they do so they are the true servants of the anonymous Christ. Salvation is not promised primarily to Christians and only tentatively extended beyond the church, as in Justin Martyr's theory of the *logos spermatikos* or Karl Rahner's thesis of the 'anonymous Christian'; salvation is simply independent of confession. Has the Gospel of Matthew made itself superfluous? Will a rereading in the light of the new disclosure be capable of resolving the dissonance?

3. The Crucified Interpreter

It would be a mistake to expect that a rereading in the light of this disclosure will be able to account tidily for every element in the Gospel of Matthew. Such an expectation would derive from a naive view of consistency and coherence which ignores the presence of difference and multiple discourses within every text. It would, again naively, attribute to the evangelist a transcendent, God-like mastery over the heterogeneous traditional material he has assembled. The most we can say is that a reading of the gospel, from the hermeneutical standpoint established by the new disclosure, may bring to light certain interpretative possibilities which would otherwise have remained unnoticed or under-emphasized. I shall outline a few of these possibilities of reading, which are to be found both in the account of Jesus' ministry to which the parable is the conclusion and in the passion narrative for which it prepares the way.

First, the possibility of a righteousness independent of any given communal and confessional context is already signalled at the outset of the Sermon on the Mount. In terms of form, the beatitudes are not imperatives but indicative statements, and their implied imperative force is dependent on their prior affirmations. When, for example, it is said, 'Blessed are those who hunger and thirst for justice, for they shall be satisfied' (5.6), the primary reference is to a form of life independent of any specific community and existent prior to the founding of the church. The implied imperative force of the beatitude serves to exhort the disciples to imitate that form of life, wherever it may be discernible.[23] Conversely, the Sermon on the Mount also speaks of the possibility of a confession that ultimately proves worthless: 'Not everyone who says to me, "Lord, Lord", shall enter the kingdom of heaven, but the one who does the will of my Father who is in heaven. On that day many will say to me, "Lord, Lord, did we not prophesy in your name, and cast out demons in your name, and do many mighty works in your name?" And then will I declare to them, "I never knew you; depart from me, you evildoers"' (7.21–23). Placing this passage alongside the beatitudes indicates that in the Sermon on the Mount the division between righteous and unrighteous is independent of any specific community and confession, just as in the parable of the sheep and the goats.

Second, the supplanting of those who say 'Lord, Lord' by those who hunger and thirst for justice is a repetition and extension of the pattern established in 8.11–12 in connection with the Gentile centurion: 'I tell you, many will come from east and west and sit at table with Abraham, Isaac and Jacob in the kingdom of heaven, while the sons of the kingdom will be thrown into the outer darkness; there people will weep and gnash their teeth.' In the first instance, this asserts the replacement of the Jewish people as a whole by a new people which includes Gentiles: 'The kingdom of God will be taken away from you and given to a nation producing the fruits of it' (21.43). Yet, as we have seen, even this new people does not coincide with the eschatological congregation of the righteous which will ultimately supplant it. 'So the last will be first, and the first last' (20.16). The children of the kingdom who are thrown into outer darkness include members of the new people no less than the old, and the criterion is the same in both cases: the accomplishment or the neglect of works of justice and mercy. Those who come from east and west to sit at table with Abraham, Isaac and Jacob include not only 'Gentile Christians' but all among the heathen who do justice and love mercy.

Third, the criterion of judgment explains how, according to Jesus, eternal life is attainable from within the communal and traditional structures of the Jewish people and without reference to himself. When asked what good deed must be done to gain eternal life, Jesus replies, openly and without reservations, 'If you would enter life, keep the commandments' (19.17b). The unexpected focus on the questioner's unremarkable use of the term 'good' – 'Why do you ask me about what is good? One there is who is good' – is intended not to pose a christological problem but to effect a transition from Jesus as the source of wisdom and insight to God, the author of the commandments. This shift from a christocentric to a theocentric perspective points the questioner back to what he already knows as a well-instructed Jew: in that, he will find the answer to his question. He must faithfully observe the commandments of the second table of the decalogue; also, far more demandingly, he must love his neighbour as himself (19.18–19). The young man claims to have observed all these commandments and seeks for some other 'good deed' that lies beyond them (19.20). The good deed that Jesus now proposes as the way to acquire treasure in heaven – 'Go, sell what you possess and give to the poor' (19.21) – is best understood not as a radical new departure but as the necessary application of the commandment of unlimited love for the neighbour. Love for the neighbour, in the concrete form of the poor, is not being expressed as the young man heaps up wealth for himself at the expense of the poor. In believing that conspicuous wealth is compatible with love for the poor neighbour (expressed perhaps in charitable works), he deceives himself; or rather, he participates in one of the characteristic illusions of his class. It is this illusion that excludes him from the eternal life attainable from within Jewish tradition when correctly understood, and not the failure to follow Jesus *per se*.

Fourth, the criterion of mercy and justice sheds light on the harsh polemic against the scribes and the Pharisees in ch.23. Here too, there is no sense of any fundamental inadequacy in Jewish tradition itself; the crowds and the disciples are exhorted to 'practise and observe whatever they tell you' (23.4). As regards their own practice, there is at least no harm in tithing mint and dill and cummin. What is disastrous, however, is the substitution of this or any other religious practice for 'the weightier matters of the law (*ta barutera tou nomou*), justice and mercy and faithfulness' (23.23). Where this occurs, religious practice becomes an ideology concealing the fact of injustice and hindering any proper response to it. A correct understanding of the Hebrew Bible would have to insist on the fundamental inseparability of the command to love the Lord our God from the command to love the neighbour: 'On these two commandments depend all the law and the prophets' (22.40). The ideology of religious practice reduces the two commandments to one, practising a love of God which overlooks the oppression of the neighbour and, in so doing, transforms the God of the oppressed into an idol which simply mirrors the religious obsessions of the isolated, abstracted self. Matthew 23 therefore need not be read as a regrettable polemic against Judaism which marks a further step along the road to a Christian anti-Semitism. As a polemic against *any* ideologizing of religious practice, it is indispensable – contrary to the characteristic liberal-ecumenical insistence that harsh language of this kind is merely the product of unfortunate and avoidable misunderstandings. A Jewish/Christian dialogue which ignores the criterion of justice, with its potential critique of current practice within both communities, serves only to obscure the most important issues (*ta barutera tou nomou*).[24]

Thus the criterion established in the parable of the sheep and the goats can be employed as a hermeneutical framework within which other elements in the Gospel of Matthew appear in a new light. In each of these cases, as in the telling of the parable, Jesus appears in the role of interpreter, and the suggestion that the hidden Christ of the parable renders the narrative of Jesus' words and deeds superfluous must now be severely qualified. If the work of justice fulfils the will of God, then the interpretative elaboration and defence of this perception is inherent to the work of justice, as is the exposure of the ideological roots of injustice. Over against any ultimate separation of deed and word, Jesus as interpreter of the will of God extends the work of justice into the ideological sphere. In the parable, Jesus appears in a dual role as the interpreter who utters it but also – in his *alter ego* as the Son of man or king – as the protagonist in the narrative. As protagonist, his role is again mainly interpretative, for the narrative is centred upon the riddle he poses as to the rationale for separation, a riddle which he solves himself when his audiences prove unable to do so. Jesus as interpreter of the will of God tells a story in which his role is doubled.

Yet, for the Gospel of Matthew, Jesus appears to be more than the interpreter of the will of God. The name 'Jesus' already indicates that 'he will save his people from their sins' (1.21); and his other name – 'Emmanuel, which means God with us' (1.22) – indicates that this salvation occurs not by words alone but by the liberating divine presence. This may help us to understand the further duality of the Son of man's role even within the parable itself: in his manifest, glorious form, he is the interpreter, but in his concealed form in secret solidarity with the oppressed he is the occasion for the actions whose performance or neglect issues in salvation or condemnation respectively. Within the parable, he is in his twofold form both the source of salvation and the interpreter of salvation, and what he interprets is his own saving presence. The oppressed, in other words, are not simply the *objects* of the work of justice – passive and as if inanimate. The Christ who has identified himself with them is no mere object but the ultimate subject, God with us in liberating grace and power. While the presence of the oppressed causes the un-righteous to close their hearts against them, to exclude them from their ways and their thoughts, it constitutes for the righteous a liberating call out of the limited sphere of personal preoccupations into the service of the God whose will must be done on earth as it is in heaven.[25] Jesus Christ in the Gospel of Matthew is not a Pelagian figment, interpreting the will of God and leaving compliance or non-compliance to the vagaries of human 'free will'. He embodies the gospel first and only then the law; only, according to the parable, he embodies both gospel and law, grace and demand, without any totalitarian requirement for explicit, exclusive adherence to his person, narrowly conceived in abstraction from the oppressed.

The hidden presence of the Son of man in solidarity with the oppressed constitutes liberating, transforming grace for the righteous; indeed, it effects their righteousness. The link between this hidden Son of man and the protagonist of the gospel narrative requires further reflection, and a clue may be found in the passage that immediately follows the conclusion of the parable. 'When Jesus had finished all these sayings, he said to his disciples, "You know that after two days the Passover is coming, and the Son of man will be delivered up to be crucified"' (26.1–2). This suffering Son of man is obviously to be identified with the Son of man in the parable, who, although he appears in glory, speaks instead of his former kenotic existence as the one who suffers in solidarity with the oppressed. The parable has the same protagonist as the passion narrative, and in both cases the theme is his suffering. In the passion narrative, this suffering is sharply focussed in the event of the crucifixion. In the preceding passage, however, the suffering of the Son of man entirely loses this sharpness of focus and this individual reference. His suffering here takes an unlimited variety of forms, for hunger, thirst, homelessness, nakedness, sickness and imprisonment are typical modes of suffering and oppression and not a complete inventory. As the suffering of the Son of man is diffused through the manifold forms and occasions of human suffering, so his individual identity disappears entirely in his anonymous, unsuspected solidarity with all the oppressed. Lest we should think of the hidden Son of man as a purely mythical figure, however, the narrator immediately proceeds to speak of the oppression of the Son of man in the most concrete political-historical terms. One of the hermeneutical functions of the parable is to interpret the passion narrative in terms of the Son of man's universal solidarity with the oppressed. Conversely, one of the hermeneutical functions of the passion narrative is to assert the historicity of oppression over against all ahistorical mythology. The Son of man has the right to identify himself with the oppressed only because he has himself suffered oppression in the concreteness of individual human existence.

How does the parable's theme of universal oppression take concrete form in the passion narrative? We recall the parable's representative list of modes of suffering: hunger, thirst, being a stranger, nakedness, sickness and imprisonment. At two points – thirst and nakedness – an immediate connection can be made with the narrative of Jesus' death. At Golgotha Jesus is thirsty: he is therefore twice offered vinegar. On the first occasion, it is mixed with *chole* – bile or bitter poison – and is therefore undrinkable (27.34): 'I was thirsty and you gave me no drink.' On the second occasion, he is able to drink the vinegar from a sponge lifted up to him on a stick (27.48): 'I was thirsty and you gave me drink.' Two of the psalms that underlie Matthew's narrative stress the sufferer's thirst. 'My strength is dried up like a potsherd, and my tongue cleaves to my jaws' (Ps. 22.15). 'For my thirst they gave me vinegar to drink' (Ps. 69.21, cf. John 19.28–30). At Golgotha Jesus is also stripped naked and publicly exposed to shame: 'I was naked and you did not clothe me' (Matt. 25.43). 'When they had crucified him, they divided his garments among them by casting lots' (27.35, cf. Ps. 22.18). Jesus' suffering is at other points analogous to the modes of suffering listed in the parable. He endures the contempt and isolation that are commonly the fate of the stranger (Matt. 27.38–44). 'Sickness' here takes the form of physical torment: 'I am poured out like water, and all my bones are out of joint' (Ps. 22.14). The physical restraint imposed by imprisonment takes a still more extreme form in the case of crucifixion. Yet it is not necessary for the Son of man to endure the precise forms of oppression listed in the parable, for the solidarity of the victims of oppression is not dependent on their enduring identical circumstances. More significant than the individual details is the common experience disclosed in the crucifixion as one of God-forsakenness: 'About the ninth hour Jesus cried with a loud voice, "Eli, Eli, lama sabachthani?", that is, "My God, my God, why hast thou forsaken me?"' (Matt. 27.46, cf. Ps. 22.1). It is his participation in this experience of total, overwhelming dispossession that makes possible the solidarity of the hidden Son of man with the victims even of forms of oppression different from his own. The cry of God-forsakenness reveals the unity of the unlimited possible experiences of oppression.

In the light of the intertextual links with the parable and with psalms that reflect the experiences of countless anonymous sufferers, we may say that the meaning of Jesus' death is to be understood in terms of the solidarity with all other victims of oppression that he here attains. Other interpretations of this event have of course multiplied from the New Testament period onwards, and these must be tested by way of this criterion of the solidarity of the oppressed. Where, for example, the cross is seen as the divine means of removing the sin which estranges God and the individual, we would have to conclude that the absence of any reference to the participation in oppression which lies at the heart of this event is an indication of an ideologizing and mythologizing tendency.[26] On the other hand, an interpretation of the crucifixion which understands it in terms of oppression does not only have a negative function in the exposure and criticism of ideology. Positively, it understands this event as giving voice to the victims of oppression, making their experience perceptible in paradigmatic form. In the light of the parable, the crucified Jesus is again the interpreter of the condition of the poor and oppressed neighbour whom the unrighteous overlook, passing by on the other side. The two roles within the parable – victim and interpreter – are here fused into one. In the parable, Jesus interprets the condition of the neighbour from a transcendent standpoint in the eschatological future, asserting his own secret presence in solidarity with him or with her. In the passion narrative, this otherwise empty claim is given credibility as he interprets the oppressed neighbour's condition from the immanent, inner-historical standpoint at which the neighbour is always located: that is, from within the place of oppression itself, where the transcendent standpoint is no longer accessible even in the imagination and where the darkness signifies the experience of being forsaken by God. Yet the purpose of this interpretation of oppression from within oppression is to evoke not simply a meditation on the mystery of a God-forsaken world but above all the hungering and thirsting for justice on which Jesus had earlier pronounced a blessing proceeding from the light of the divine future. The crucified Jesus does not offer a mere *explanation* of the world; dis-illusionment stemming from the exposure of the harshness of reality is not an end in itself, for he is the source of liberating grace and not the manifestation of an inexorable law. This liberation is the freeing of the Samaritan to fulfil his vocation to be a neighbour: its source is the wounded, naked figure at the roadside, and its ultimate horizon is the kingdom of God in which the hunger and thirst for justice will be satisfied. This interpretation of reality, which aims at the transformation of reality, is also to be found in the parable of the sheep and the goats. Its theme is not law but grace; a grace that has no existence apart from the praxis evoked by the oppressed neighbour who is its proximate source.

In attempting an exegesis open to the concerns of theologies of liberation, I have made eclectic use of a number of the hermeneutical and exegetical strategies currently available. I have at one point or another appealed to the implied reader, to the interpretative freedom of the actual reader, to the poststructuralist emphasis on indeterminacy and intertextuality, to feminist analysis of androcentric language, and to certain elements in the practice of narrative criticism. In subjecting this medley of interpretative strategies to an overarching theological problematic, I have sought to resist the tendency to work, so far as possible, within the confines of a self-contained textuality abstracted from the contemporary sociopolitical contexts in which it in fact operates. Just as there is no self-contained text devoid of multiple intertextual relationships with other texts, so there is no text which is not intricately bound up with practices and ideologies which are ultimately *extra-textual*: not only in the sense that they may be encountered outside written texts, but also in the sense that the labyrinthine interpretative subtleties currently associated with the notion of textuality may at certain critical junctures be wholly inappropriate. At certain points, in other words, a decision imposes itself for one option and against another. An opposition is established between what asserts itself to be truth and what is alleged to be falsehood, and this opposition will not readily submit to deconstructive dissolution. The subjection of interpretative pluralism to theological, ethical and political constraints places a question-mark against the current tendency to celebrate an allegedly free, innocent proliferation of meaning. Our increasing sense of the multiplicity of interpretative possibilities must be tempered by a willingness to articulate ethically defensible interpretative goals.

Notes

1. See, for example, N.K. Gottwald, *The Tribes of Yahweh*, Maryknoll: Orbis Books and London: SCM Press 1979; *The Hebrew Bible: A Socio-Literary Introduction*, Philadelphia: Fortress Press 1985; C. Myers, *Binding the Strong Man: A Political Reading of Mark's Story of Jesus*, Maryknoll: Orbis Books 1988; D. Rensberger, *Overcoming the World: Politics and Community in the Gospel of John*, London: SPCK 1988; C. Rowland and M. Corner, *Liberating Exegesis. The Challenge of Liberation Theology to Biblical Studies*, London: SPCK 1990.
2. But note also the exegetical work of J.S. Croatto, J.P. Miranda, G. Pixley and E. Tamez.
3. C. Mesters, *Defenseless Flower. A New Reading of the Bible*, ET Maryknoll: Orbis Books 1989, 99.
4. C. Boff, *Theology and Praxis: Epistemological Foundations*, ET Maryknoll: Orbis Books 1987, 132–58. Boff is concerned to establish the continuity of biblical interpretation within the base communities with the inner-biblical process of tradition, in opposition to the notion of a one-to-one correspondence between contemporary situations and situations in biblical times.
5. Compare the comments of R.S. Sugirtharajah on the way in which biblical scholarship has largely confined the production of knowledge to 'male Euro-American scholars' (in R.S. Sugirtharajah (ed.), *Voices from the Margin: Interpreting the Bible in the Third World*, London: SPCK 1991, 2).
6. This is the significance of G. Gutiérrez's stress on the comprehensive unity of human history, in opposition to 'those who, in order to protect salvation (or to protect their interests) lift salvation from the midst of history, where individuals and social classes struggle to liberate themselves from the slavery and oppression to which other individuals and social classes have subjected them' (*A Theology of Liberation*, ET Maryknoll: Orbis Books 1973; London: SCM Press 1974, 104).
7. Gutiérrez points out that the restoration of 'democracy' and 'human rights' may 'alleviate the most blatant forms of repression' without

touching the institutionalized violence which perpetuates 'the misery and spoliation of the poorest of the poor' (*The Power of the Poor in History*, ET Maryknoll: Orbis Books and London: SCM Press 1983, 87).

8. See note 1 above, Gottwald's work is applied in a black South African context by I.J. Mosala, *Biblical Hermeneutics and Black Theology in South Africa*, Grand Rapids: Eerdmans 1990.

9. See note 6 above.

10. In a survey of the history of interpretation, S.W. Gray shows that historically the restricted reading has predominated; only in the twentieth century has the comprehensive interpretation of the *adelphoi* become common (*The Least of my Brothers. Matthew 25:31–46: A History of Interpretation*, SBL Dissertation Series 114, Atlanta, Georgia: Scholars Press 1987, 348). Calvin's view is typical: 'Believers only are expressly recommended to us; not that [Christ] bids us altogether to despise others, but because the more closely a man approaches God, the more highly he should be esteemed by us. Though there is a common tie that binds all the children of Adam, there is a still more sacred union among the children of God' (as quoted by Gray, 208).

11. For a useful statement of the case for the restricted reading, see J. Mánek, 'Mit wem identifiziert sich Jesus? Eine exegetische Rekonstruktion ad Matt. 25:31–46', in B. Lindars and S.S. Smalley (ed.), *Christ and Spirit in the New Testament*, Cambridge: Cambridge University Press 1973, 15–25. Mánek implies that this reading *enhances* the theological value of the passage: 'Das Verhalten, das seine Motivierung im Mitleid hat, ist sicher wertvoll, aber es ist noch wertvoller, wenn es mit Hilfe der Verkündigung Christi verbunden ist' (25). Other presentations of the restricted reading are cited by E. Schweizer in G.N. Stanton (ed.), *The Interpretation of Matthew*, London: SPCK and Philadelphia: Fortress Press 1983, 152 n. 54.

12. For the Matthean usage of the term 'brother', see J. Friedrich, *Gott im Bruder? Eine methodenkritische Untersuchung von Redaktion, Überlieferung und Traditionen in Mt 25,31–46*, Calwer Theologische Monographien, Stuttgart: Calwer Verlag, 1977, 220–39: in v.40, *adelphos* is probably redactional and refers to the church member (238–39). Friedrich claims that it is consistent with Matthew's emphasis on the church 'dass er die Frage nach dem Gericht über die Heiden ausschliesslich aus dem Blickwinkel der Gemeinde und von daher die Heiden aufgrund ihres Verhaltens den Christen gegenüber gerichtet sieht' (266). In its present form, the passage reassures the Matthean community, during a period of Gentile persecution, 'dass all das, was durch die Heiden an den Gemeindegliedern positiv oder negativ getan wurde, alleiniger Masstab beim Endgericht über eben diese Heiden sein würde' (267). The comprehensive reference of *elachistoi*, originally intended by

Jesus, was restricted by Matthew's insertion of 'brothers' (248–49); this restricted meaning was anticipated by radical Jewish Christian 'Wanderprediger', who applied the former term to themselves (277).

13. Compare J. Mánek, 'Mit wem identifiziert sich Jesus?', 19, emphasizing the significance of II Cor. 11.

14. G.N. Stanton identifies the 'brothers' as 'those sent out by Matthew's community as missionaries "to all nations"'. Experiencing opposition to their message, Matthean Christians ask why God permits this to occur, and 25.31–46 gives the answer (cf. IV Ezra 7.37 and II Baruch 72): 'At the end all men will certainly be judged, rewarded and punished on the basis of their acceptance or rejection of Christian missionaries' ('The Gospel of Matthew and Judaism', *BJRL* 66 [1984], 264–84, 280). Compare his more detailed discussion of this passage in *A Gospel for a New People*, Edinburgh: T. & T. Clark 1992, 207–31.

15. H. Räisänen, *Beyond New Testament Theology: A Story and a Programme*, London: SCM Press and Philadelphia: Trinity Press International 1990, 136.

16. E. Schweizer believes that the commandment in 5.43–48 to love one's enemies makes the restrictive reading improbable: 'Elitism is the possible meaning here; but more likely Matthew construes the words of the Judge in a broader sense' (*The Good News according to Matthew*, ET Atlanta: John Knox Press 1975; London: SPCK 1976, 479. The weakness of such attempts to refute the restrictive reading by conventional exegetical means indicates that the issue is primarily a hermeneutical one.

17. Thus F. Gogarten appeals to Matt. 25.31–46 in support of his privileging of 'the world of each individual' over 'the ordinary world of history' (*Christ the Crisis*, ET London: SCM Press 1970, 179). 'In Jesus' preaching my 'neighbour' is the person who on any particular occasion is close to me in an exclusive sense, and towards whom I have to act in such a way that by comparison everything else with which I have to do, that is, everything in the world in general, ... fades into insignificance' (180). The abstraction of self and neighbour from the history that has, in fact, brought the relationship into existence serves only to conceal the truth about this relationship. Unfortunately, there is nothing in Matt. 25.31–46 that resists such a reading.

18. See J.P. Miranda, *Communism in the Bible*, ET Maryknoll: Orbis Books and London: SCM Press 1982, 21–56.

19. As W. Grundmann notes, 'der Ton liegt ... nicht auf einer Gerichtsverhandlung, sondern auf der Verkündigung des endgültigen Urteils und seiner Begründung vor den durch dieses überraschten Menschen' (*Das Evangelium nach Matthäus*, Theologischer Handkommentar zum Neuen Testament I, Berlin: Evangelische Verlagsanstalt 1968, 524).

20. In Wolfgang Iser's theory of reading, it is the multiple possibility of connecting one part of the text with another that establishes textual indeterminacy and the active co-operation of the reader in the production of meaning. This explains how 'the same intersubjective structure of the literary text may give rise to so many different subjective realizations' (*The Act of Reading: A Theory of Aesthetic Response*, Baltimore: Johns Hopkins University Press 1978, 118). This theory of the *act* of reading by an actual reader may be differentiated from a theory of an 'implied reader' located wholly within the text; compare Seymour Chatman's narrative communication model, in which the communication of a real author with a real reader takes place only by way of surrogates with no existence outside the text (*Story and Discourse: Narrative Structure in Fiction and Film*, Ithaca: Cornell University Press 1978, 151).

21. On this point see L. Boff, *Jesus Christ Liberator: A Critical Christology for our Time*, Maryknoll: Orbis Books 1978; London: SPCK 1980, 95; J. Cone, *A Black Theology of Liberation*, Maryknoll: Orbis Books 1986², 134–35. C. Boff refers to this passage in support of his view of Christianity as 'the *interpretation* of the salvation of the world, and not the salvation of the world itself, or even the exclusive instrument of this salvation' (*Theology and Praxis*, 98).

22. Bonhoeffer, on the other hand, reads Matt. 25.31–46 as a statement about the 'good works' of Christians, secretly accomplished through them by God: 'Great will be our astonishment in that day, and we shall then realize that it is not our works which remain, but the work which God has wrought through us in his good time without any effort of will and intention on our part' (*The Cost of Discipleship*, ET London: SCM Press 1948, 268). The concern with the relationship of justification and sanctification here obscures the primacy of the encounter with the poor and oppressed, which Bonhoeffer does not mention.

23. It is not sufficient simply to point to the parenetic function of the third person plural form of the Matthean beatitudes (U. Luz, *Matthew 1–7: A Commentary*, ET Minneapolis: Augsburg Fortress 1989; Edinburgh: T. and T. Clark 1990, 228). In the narrative context of 5.1–2, the use of third person rather than second person forms in 5.3–10 has the effect of differentiating the addressees (the disciples) from those upon whom the blessings are pronounced. The shift to the second person plural in vv.11–12 indicates for the first time that the relationship of the disciples to Jesus may be located within the broader setting portrayed in the preceding verses.

24. According to the Jewish liberation theologian Marc H. Ellis, 'The implicit or explicit theology brought to these dialogues from the Jewish side is a Holocaust theology that centers on empowerment and support

of Israel. To be in good faith the Christian dialogue partners must first and foremost signal their wholehearted assent, and any vacillation is equated with anti-Semitism ... [On the other hand,] a true Jewish liberationist believes that Palestine and the support of a Palestinian state formed by the Palestine Liberation Organization need to be part of any discussion of Israel and thus part of the ecumenical dialogue' (*Toward a Jewish Theology of Liberation*, Maryknoll: Orbis Books 1987; London: SCM Press 1988, 120.

25. Compare Elsa Tamez's discussion of the biblical concept of 'conversion', in *Bible of the Oppressed*, ET Maryknoll: Orbis Books 1982, 75–82.
26. See, for example, Jon Sobrino's criticisms of the Anselmian theory of atonement (*Christology at the Crossroads: A Latin American View*, Maryknoll: Orbis Books and London: SCM Press 1978, 192–93).

4

After Hermeneutics: The Relationship between Theology and Biblical Studies

Werner G. Jeanrond

Hermeneutics, the study of proper means of text-interpretation, is not the cause of the current crisis in biblical studies, rather it may point indirectly to some ways out of this crisis. Of course, it is true to say that hermeneutics has destroyed the claims to any total objectivity in biblical interpretation, theology and any other discipline of human knowledge. But hermeneutics has equally invalidated the pretensions of any purely subjectivist approach to biblical texts, i.e. approaches based on nothing other than the conviction that one's preferred theory of what the biblical text ought to say or stand for is just fine. Thus, it has become obvious that neither objectivist nor subjectivist ideologies of reading have helped the critical reader any further in her or his attempt to understand the potential of meaning in biblical texts, or indeed any other written or oral texts.

Moreover, the lack of proper integration of biblical and theological studies in most faculties of theology has long been a cause for grave concern for some teachers and many students. The uncertainty as to the ultimate purpose of biblical studies is, I think, the main reason for the current crisis of self-understanding of this academic discipline. What can the study of the Bible offer to the diverse interests of students late in the twentieth century? What is the contribution of biblical studies to the academy, to society at large and to the different Jewish and Christian communities? In other words, what is the discipline of biblical studies good for these days? The Conference on 'New Directions for Biblical Studies?' for which this paper was originally written stressed both the urgency of this

85

search for a new purpose of biblical studies and the need to reflect upon the context in which this search takes place. Should biblical scholars write more commentaries or should they give more consideration to the readers' experiences of the biblical texts and to the diversity of particular aims of reading? Should biblical criticism become more user-friendly and therefore give some renewed consideration to the intellectual and spiritual milieu in which it operates?

In this paper I wish to pursue these questions with particular regard to the possibilities of a better relationship between biblical and theological studies, in the light of recent insights into hermeneutics. In a first historical section, I shall examine some of the effects of hermeneutics on the theologian's view of contemporary biblical studies. The second, more systematic section is devoted to the need for a new kind of theological approach to the Bible. In the third and more practical section I shall examine ways of revising our research strategies and of reorganizing the labour in our theological faculties accordingly. In my concluding remarks I shall point to the limits of such a new biblical theology. My overall thesis is that we urgently require a new kind of biblical theology, and I understand this paper as a proposal towards that goal.

After Hermeneutics: The Many Purposes of Biblical Interpretation

1. The limits of historical-critical scholarship

In times of crisis it may be helpful to engage in some historical reflection in order to ascertain what brought the crisis about in the first place. That there is something markedly wrong with traditional historical-critical scholarship of the Bible has been clear for some time. Karl Barth perhaps expressed this concern best when in 1922 in the preface to his *The Epistle to the Romans* he demanded that the historical-critical exegetes ought to be more critical[1]. And it was precisely the fact that Barth did not produce yet another philologically oriented commentary on the text but a particular reading from a very definite theological perspective which illustrated his new approach to biblical scholarship. He wanted biblical exegetes to return to what he perceived to be their proper vocation, namely to serve the development of a biblically grounded Christian theology.

However, that was exactly what biblical thinkers wanted to avoid. They did not want to lose their scientific autonomy and academic self-esteem, developed in reaction to the uncritical attempts by anti-Enlightenment church leaders and church people alike to fight the influence of a critical study of the text. Thus, the need to defend the critical reading of the scriptures lies at the heart of the modern self-understanding of biblical scholarship; and who would want to deny either the great success of that tradition of biblical studies or the enormous insights into the historical continuities and discontinuities of the early Christian movement which historical-critical research has produced?

But in our time this kind of approach to the Bible came under renewed attack from two different sides at once. On the one hand, theologians such as Barth expressed their critique of the limited scope of a merely historically-minded biblical interpretation, and, on the other hand, the development of philosophical hermeneutics provided a radical challenge to the very nature of the historicist tradition of biblical scholarship. Hermeneutical thinking placed a large question-mark against the claims to objectivity, neutrality and autonomy of the modern reader. Thus, while Barth demanded that historical-critical exegetes ought to be more critical in terms of recognizing and responding to the theological perspectives of their textual objects, philosophical hermeneuts pointed out that the very method of traditional historical-critical biblical scholarship was flawed. It was neither sufficiently critical nor self-critical.

In response to the demands for a methodological reorientation, the discussion on adequate approaches to the Bible has taken many turns. The defenders of a purist historical-critical approach to the study of the scriptures have seen themselves confronted by a host of new attempts to approach the Bible from literary, sociological, psychological, canonical, feminist, liberationist, structuralist and deconstructionist perspectives. All aspects of critical attention which are applied to the reading of literary texts have now also been tried in efforts to interpret the Bible. But rather than dealing with the dilemma of alleviating the fundamental crisis of historical-critical scholarship of the Bible the development and application of all these new approaches to the biblical texts have increased further the urgency to ascertain why and for whom biblical scholars actually work. The shift, for instance, from a historical towards a literary study of the scriptures does not answer the question for whom this kind of interpretation is actually intended. Is it *l'art pour l'art*? Does the result of this kind of biblical scholarship benefit anybody directly or indirectly? This brings us back to Barth's question. Does not biblical scholarship at some point have to address the theological dimensions of the biblical texts? However, Barth's view of the exclusively Christian significance of biblical scholarship cannot be defended any longer today. Rather, the necessity of approaching the scriptures from a variety of view-points has been strongly supported by contemporary hermeneutical theory. Thus, the question today is not whether everybody must interpret the Bible theologically, but whether one can claim to have done justice to the semantic potential of the biblical texts without attending to the theological nature of these texts.

While it is perfectly possible and legitimate to treat the Bible as an object for all kinds of specialized readings and investigations, some form of a theological reading of the scriptures, though not necessarily according to the ecclesial lines suggested by Barth, is imperative for any critical reader of the biblical texts who wishes to respond more fully to their semantic potential. It is important to note that I am not arguing here that only professional theologians are in a position to develop adequate strategies of biblical interpretation. However, I am arguing that the biblical texts themselves offer theological perspectives to the reader which a reader who claims to respond to the texts' own communicative perspectives cannot afford to ignore. By 'theological perspective' I mean that these texts raise in their different ways the question of God.

Before I treat of this point in more detail I would like, however, to sketch very briefly and from a theological perspective the impact of hermeneutical thinking on the relationship between theological and biblical thinking in this century.

2. *The impact of philosophical hermeneutics on the theological view of the relationship between theological and biblical studies*

Until and including Friedrich Schleiermacher most professional interpreters of biblical texts were concerned with interpretation theory, i.e. with hermeneutics. Famous interpreters of the scriptures such as Origen, Jerome, Augustine, Thomas Aquinas, Luther, Calvin, Spinoza, Semler, and Schleiermacher all found it necessary to engage in some form of explicit and critical reflection on the method of biblical interpretation. The matrix of the hermeneutical orientation of these people was largely determined by the ancient debates on whether the biblical interpreter should engage in literal or in allegorical reading, or more precisely, to what extent one should follow the one or the other and whether some combination of both was desirable. This natural inclination of biblical interpreters to concern themselves with questions of hermeneutics, which these Christian thinkers had in common with many of their Jewish and Islamic colleagues, got lost after Schleiermacher. While philosophers such as Dilthey, Husserl, Wach, Heidegger, Gadamer, Ricoeur and Derrida have continued the search for proper theories of text-interpretation, Christian theologians in general and Christian exegetes in particular developed a strong preference for the historical-critical method of reading the Bible and until recently left the further development of hermeneutical theory to philosophers and literary critics.

In view of their academic context, i.e. the particular division of labour in theological faculties, exegetes could pursue their philological and historical examinations of the biblical texts with a silent confidence that their colleagues in systematic and practical theology would pay proper attention to the overall theological meaning of these texts and to the results of their particular exegetical investigations. Moreover, the academic milieu in which, for instance, New Testament exegetes such as Schlatter, Käsemann, Barrett, Dodd, Hengel, Dunn and H.D. Betz have been working has retained a generally positive attitude towards Christian interests, so that the work of these scholars has been guaranteed some form of a Christian reception and integration, at least by those of their colleagues in systematic theology who have continued to share an interest in the historical understanding of the scriptures. However, the larger non-theological public within and outside of the academy has long since given up following the detailed philological and historical work of biblical scholars and appears utterly surprised when occasionally fragments of their insights are drawn to its attention. The split between popular biblical piety on the one hand and the guild of biblical scholars on the other hand is at least as great today as it was in the later Middle Ages.

Robert Morgan and John Barton are, of course, correct when they insist that historical scholarship, too, fulfils a valuable function in so far as it can register a protest against the theological domestication of biblical texts by modern readers.[2] But how often do we hear such necessary public protests by exegetes? Does not such a protest presuppose that exegetes follow the theological as well as the wider intellectual and praxis-oriented discourse on the Bible?

In our century, there have been three prominent attempts by theologians to lead biblical scholarship out of its self-imposed isolation, and, with the help of philosophical hermeneutics, to reconnect it to the larger theological question of how the Bible mediates ultimate meaning to its readers. These three attempts can be easily identified through their major protagonists. The first effort in this century to benefit from philosophical hermeneutics for a theological reading of scriptures was made by Rudolf Bultmann, the second by the promoters of the so-called 'New Hermeneutic', and the third attempt to develop a new biblical theology is under way at present.[3] In the remainder of this historical section I wish to discuss briefly the first two approaches to biblical theology; and in the following systematic section propose a more adequate method for a theological interpretation of the scriptures.

In response to Martin Heidegger's early hermeneutics of *Dasein*, Rudolf Bultmann developed his own version of an existentially focussed biblical theology. He was very much aware of the need for a critical hermeneutics in biblical text-interpretation, and demanded in particular a clarification of the presuppositions through which the modern interpreter approaches the biblical text. This hermeneutical reflection, regarded by Barth as an unjustifiable philosophical imposition on the biblical text, was considered by Bultmann to be a necessary methodological move which alone could open the possibility of a genuine understanding of the biblical text. Thus, by insisting that any act of biblical interpretation must be assessed in the light of the best available hermeneutical insights, Bultmann reconnected biblical interpretation and theology with the great hermeneutical tradition lost to theology since Schleiermacher's death.

> [N]o exegesis is without presuppositions, inasmuch as the exegete is not a *tabula rasa*, but on the contrary, approaches the text with specific questions or with a specific way of raising questions and thus has a certain idea of the subject matter with which the text is concerned.[4]

Bultmann identified the question of God in the horizon of his time as the perspective which guided the reading of the New Testament, and then linked the modern existential quest for God with the particular historical answer to this quest in the scriptures. Even if today we detect in Bultmann's proposal an individualist reduction, and even if we can no longer agree with the terminology of demythologizing the New Testament, Bultmann's crucial insights into the nature of the interpretative process remain valid: a biblical text speaks only to a person who can approach it with a question. Moreover, Bultmann's hermeneutical move was not really directed against historical understanding, as is often claimed, but against the objectivist pretensions of some historical scholarship. The implications and limitations of historical thinking had to be properly grasped. That is why Bultmann emphasized so forcefully that we today cannot live the life of first-century Christians. Instead we have to translate the christological experiences and message of our Christian predecessors into our own language. Interpretation is our only access to the biblical texts.

In spite of Bultmann's shortcomings, such as the existentialist reduction, the opposition between myth and kerygma, and the failure to engage in a critical reflection on the nature of language, Bultmann's lasting achievement remains his insight into the necessity of hermeneutical reflection in biblical interpretation and theology.[5]

Ernst Fuchs, Gerhard Ebeling, James M. Robinson, Robert W. Funk and other representatives of the New Hermeneutic, the second attempt to relate philosophical hermeneutics and biblical interpretation in this century, pay more attention to the problem of language than Bultmann did. They followed the later Heidegger's invitation to listen again to the words of great literature, to those instances where the call of Being could be heard. The representatives of the New Hermeneutic therefore recommended that the reader of the biblical texts listen anew to the voice of Being expressed in these texts. The New Testament helps us to recover our language. Ernst Fuchs put it like this:

> So we must find out to what extent our mental activity, our seeing, is bound to a hearing. That is the hermeneutical problem. It is posed for us every day anew. This is the point of departure for the New Testament.[6]

As a result Fuchs proposed a hermeneutics of agreement with the biblical text, a hermeneutics of faith.[7]

Gerhard Ebeling has gone one step further and connected the new insights into hermeneutics with the Reformation tradition. He regrets the only limited hermeneutical awareness of the Reformers, yet sets out to redeem their insight into the Word event now with the help of twentieth-century hermeneutical sophistication. Thus, he can define the purpose of hermeneutics like this:

> The aim of such interpretation cannot, however, be anything other than the removal of the obstacle which prevents the Word from mediating understanding itself.[8]

Thus, Ebeling's concern with hermeneutics stands firmly in the service of his intentions to make reformational theology of the Word respectable in modern times. His and Fuchs' theological reading of the scriptures are thus not open-ended endeavours motivated by a search for a new and always better understanding of what the biblical texts have to say about God, anthropology and eschatology, but attempts to stabilize particular sets of traditional theological interpretations of the Bible.

I must say that I can understand the reluctance of biblical scholars to subscribe to the methodology of the New Hermeneutic. In principle not unlike older attempts to read a set of doctrinal convictions back into the scriptures, the New Hermeneutic developed a new form of doctrinal interpretation. Whereas Bultmann adopted a philosophical perspective for his reading of the scriptures, advocates of the New Hermeneutic used a philosophical insight into language to vindicate their particular reformational theologies. Ultimately both attempts to relate theological and biblical studies have to fail: Bultmann's existentialist-philosophical starting-point does not provide us with a wide enough reading perspective, and the Fuchs-Ebeling tradition only discovered what their reformational theology, now hermeneutically upgraded, allowed them to see. Neither approach helps us then to overcome the old dilemma in biblical interpretation, namely that theologians tend to distort the Bible by reading it dogmatically and biblical scholars tend to study the Bible as history or literature. Is there an alternative to both of these reductions, i.e. the dogmatic on the one hand, and the historical-critical or literary reading on the other hand?

The Possibility of a New Biblical Theology

Three in particular of the recent debates in hermeneutics seem to me to be of great importance for any reflection on the appropriateness of biblical interpretation: (1) the debate on method in text-interpretation, (2) the debate on adequate models of interaction between text and reading, and (3) the debate on praxis. Let me briefly comment on each of these and then proceed to develop some aspects of a critical biblical theology.

1. The debate on method in text-interpretation

In response to Hans-Georg Gadamer's idealist vision, according to which truth manifests itself to every well-intentioned reader of a classic text without any need for an explicit method of interpretation, both Jürgen Habermas and Paul Ricoeur have defended the need for method in text-interpretation. They have pointed to the ubiquity of ideological distortions in human communication and called therefore for a thorough mode of ideology critique in every act of reading. Thus, as Ricoeur insists, a host of explanatory moves are necessary in order to check, validate and, where necessary, correct our first understanding of a text. No interpretation of the meaning of a complex literary text can ever claim to be final. Rather the preunderstandings of a particular interpreter which provide the necessary starting-point for any interpretative act, are in constant need of critique and revision.[9] While Gadamer trusts blindly in the self-purifying nature of interpretative processes, Ricoeur and Habermas emphasize the need for suspicion in every act of interpretation. For both philosophers a retrieval of a text's meaning must always be accompanied by suspicion. And in the same spirit, the interpretative process as a whole is therefore best located in a community of interpreters in which these necessary checks can be performed and the always preliminary results of any interpretative action assessed.

Especially those communities which see themselves as largely determined by the 'proper' understanding of certain canonical texts, such as the Jewish or the Christian movements, require such means of correction and validation. Totalitarian fixations arising from one particular interpretation stifle this hermeneutical process, and, if undetected, as in the case of the various patriarchal fixations in Christianity, succeed in persisting for centuries.

As this debate on method has clearly shown, only a pluralistic approach to our canonical texts guarantees the possibility of developing ever more adequate interpretations and of detecting open and hidden ideologies. In the case of biblical interpretation, a pluralistic reading of the Bible and a rigorous examination both of the text and of particular acts of reading offer the best guarantee against renewed efforts to reduce the Bible to a mere collection of proof-texts for one theological argument or another.

2. *The interaction of text and reading*

One of the great achievements of the continuing debate on adequate modes of reading has been the emphasis on the dynamic nature both of the text and of the act of reading. Neither the text nor any reading can be treated as static entities, rather the semantic unity of any given text can unfold itself only in the act of reading itself – and that means only because of the involvement of a reader or a group of readers. The debate on exactly how much the text determines the act of reading and to what extent the reader determines the meaning of the text continues. Few people, however, seriously question any longer the fact that both parties are involved, and that therefore any interpretation of a text is the result of an interplay between text and reader. This dynamic and interactive nature of interpretation does not mean that there can only be subjective readings, rather it means that we have to continue to search for the best insights into how objective we can consider an interpretation to be and how much involvement of the reading subject is necessary. Thus, the time of the monarchical rule of either formalism or reader-response-criticism is over, and the time of their mutually critical interplay has finally begun.[10]

With regard to biblical interpretation, this discussion offers us an emphatic reminder that no reading can be considered appropriate which remains uninvolved with the text. Once again, any objectivist tendencies of historical-critical research are shattered, but so are all other calls for monistic readings of the biblical texts, be they theological, liberationist, feminist, ecclesialist, traditionalist, or whatever. Monism is never a promising avenue in the search for more adequate approaches to texts.

Moreover, the recent contribution to hermeneutics by text-linguistics has shown that the textuality of a text is the result of an interplay of different communicative perspectives. That the text is a structured whole, Schleiermacher already knew and said. But that the text is a highly complex network of interconnected themes and rhemes (i.e. of communications and their progressive qualification) is an insight which we owe in particular to the Prague School of linguistics.[11] The analysis by the reader of the particular themes and rhemes which form the communicative perspective of a text allows the classification of texts in terms of their genres as predominantly aesthetic, legal, political, religious, theological, and so on. Moreover, once such a determination of a text's genre has been established and subjected to all available forms of critical checks, the reader will be in a position to develop his or her reading genres accordingly.

In the case of biblical interpretation, it will be crucial to identify the particular genre of the different texts in order to assess which genre of reading will be most appropriate to these texts. This is not to say that one could not study, let us say, the historical, literary, philosophical, ethnic, aesthetic and indeed any other perspective which may also be part of a biblical text's overall composition. Yet I cannot accept claims that any such limited reading genre represents a full reading of the biblical text. If the primary genre of the biblical texts is considered to be theological because all of these texts reflect on the nature of God and on God's relationship with humankind, then these texts ultimately demand a theological reading.

3. The praxis of contextual reading

The debate on the relationship between hermeneutics and praxis is of importance to our discussion because it highlights the contextual dimension of all acts of interpretation. The question which animates this debate relates to what is primary in text-interpretation: on the one hand, the concern for adequacy in theory which helps us to understand and then possibly transform our praxis, or, on the other hand, the concerns of a particular praxis out of which the questions have arisen which are then put to the text in the act of reading. For instance, does a genuine concern for Christian liberative praxis in Latin America and elsewhere necessarily lead to a better (i.e. emancipatory) reading of the scriptures than the theory-laden approaches to the Bible in the First World? In other words, does the interpreter of the Bible need to pass the test of whatever counts as the proper interpretative inclination in order to be able to disclose the corresponding truth of the text? Or should any kind of presupposition, however worthy, be submitted to the ideology test as demanded by Ricoeur and Habermas?

I do not see any difficulty with the demand that all approaches to the biblical texts should be rooted in a certain praxis; Gadamer too spoke of the need to approach the text with our particular prejudices, though he demanded that these prejudices be tested and if need be transformed in the act of reading itself. Nor do I have any difficulty in accepting that Christian theology ought to be formulated as a theory for concrete Christian praxis; that position was already maintained by Schleiermacher. But I do have a serious problem with the demand that one or the other particular conviction should determine (rather than condition) our approach to the Bible. Though for different reasons, such a predetermination of our reading would lead to a prison similar to the one in which Fuchs and Ebeling, and to a lesser extent Bultmann, would have liked to see us, namely the demand for a correct theological starting-point which alone can authenticate the subsequent reading of the Bible. However, no reading perspective can be accepted if it is not first put to the test in the act of reading itself. It would be rather paradoxical if new and important insights into the meaning of the biblical texts, such as the insight into God's commitment to the liberation of men, women and children from all kinds of oppression, would now be allowed to terminate the further exploration of the meaning of these texts by attempting to control the development of new and different perspectives. Having overcome the doctrinal reading of the Bible from the past, it would be a pity for us now to become a victim of new and hidden doctrinaire positions in biblical interpretation.

4. The possibility of a new biblical theology

The three hermeneutical debates which I have mentioned do not in my opinion rule out the possibility of a new and different biblical theology. Rather, they help to dismantle wrong and inadequate expectations invested in a specifically theological approach to the Bible. Once we have ruled out any form of doctrinal reading of the Bible and put in place proper safeguards against ideological readings of the text, we are in a better position to read the Bible with a view to doing justice to its complex and at times even contradictory theological potential.

Our theological interest in the Bible is not only not alien to these texts, rather it has been kindled in part by these texts themselves and in part by the Jewish and Christian communities who consider these texts to be normative for present and future reflection on God and on God's relationship to this world. However, as we have seen, the biblical texts in their diversity were not always given the opportunity to reveal the plurality of their perspectives on God and on God's relationship with this universe, and on the plurality of positive and negative human responses to God's offer of relationship. Rather, theological systems and constructs have at times, in fact most of the time, been used to isolate and emphasize one particular tradition or subcanon within the Bible or one biblical text's perspective to the detriment of other equally important texts and textual perspectives. And at times all biblical perspectives on God were put under the control of a particular male interest group in the synagogues and churches.

In this connection it is also of interest that previous attempts at formulating biblical theologies, such as those of Bultmann and Conzelmann, and hermeneutically inspired readings of the scriptures, such as those of the scholars promoting the New Hermeneutic, have by and large ignored the Old Testament and thus tended to isolate the Christian reflection on God from its own Jewish background.

In view of these developments I wish to propose that we reread the biblical texts with the aim of establishing more fully the diversity of theological reflection in these writings without, however, the doctrinal obsession to systematize everything. Such a theological reading of the scriptures, seeking to be enlightened by all the efforts of biblical scholarship, would be able to combine the ancient Christian tradition of a theological reading of the scriptures with the modern and postmodern hermeneutical strategies of retrieval and suspicion. Moreover, it could free the many biblical scholars of today whose self-understanding suffers from a crisis of purpose to contribute constructively to the development of a truly critical and never final biblical theology. This project could also help Christian systematic theologians to test their understanding of the biblical approaches to God thoroughly against the texts themselves and to appreciate better the diversity of biblical reflection on God, on human nature and history, and on the meaning and purpose of this world.

The strategies of critique developed in order to detect hidden and open ideologies in the process of reading must, of course, not only be applied to the acts of reading but also to the texts themselves, which may also contain hidden and open ideologies. That such ideological dimensions are in fact present in the texts of the Bible has been made particularly evident by the feminist critique. More than any other critical approach, it has been this that has drawn our attention to the fact that both the biblical texts and their readers require constant critical attention.

However, the present structure of our biblical and theological work in the academy does not yet really promote such a theological approach to the biblical texts. Let me therefore comment briefly at this point on the academic context of such a project of biblical theology.

The Need for a Reform of the Theological Curriculum

The split between biblical and theological studies in our usual university curriculum dates back as far as the scholastic reform of theological studies in the Middle Ages. Thomas Aquinas set out to explain *sacra scriptura* in his *sacra doctrina*. But contrary to this intention, *sacra doctrina* developed quite independently from the scriptures. The theologians expected from their exegetical colleagues that they produce a trustworthy text and relevant philological notes on the texts (glosses and sentences), while they, the theologians, employed grand philosophical schemes in order to develop their own theological systems, though still claiming that these schemes interpreted the scriptures. Although in a certain limited way that claim was correct, both groups had little to say to each other. Only the Reformers' concern with the scriptures produced a new co-operation between biblical and theological interests, but the heirs of the Reformers either embarked on metaphysical journeys as eagerly as their Roman Catholic counterparts did, or reduced the interpretation of the scriptures to fit the particular Reformation doctrines of biblical interpretation.

Early in the nineteenth century Friedrich Schleiermacher proposed a new integrated theological theory for Christian praxis by designing a curriculum of studies which was divided into three parts: a first, philosophical part in which the foundations of apologetics and polemics were discussed, followed secondly by a historical part which included exegesis, church history, dogmatic theology and church statistics (by the latter he meant a discussion of the corporate constitution of Christian community), and thirdly a practical part which dealt with church service and church government.[12]

Although this proposal cannot do justice to our needs and our understanding of Christian praxis today, it is of interest to us in so far as it integrates biblical and dogmatic concerns, in this case under 'historical theology'. But as we saw above, Schleiermacher's hermeneutical grasp of the need to bring biblical and theological concerns more closely together was lost after his death.

In view of the new hermeneutical connection between biblical studies and theological studies today, it seems not to be a premature proposal to suggest a reorganization of the division of labour in our theological faculties and schools. Of course, there will always be an interest in studying the Bible as a historical and literary document of classical status outside the confessional Jewish or Christian context. However, within the context of Christian theology biblical and theological labours have to be much more closely integrated. It simply does not make sense that theologians today are not actively engaged in studying the primary texts of their traditions, while their biblical colleagues are on the whole not involved in discussing the intellectual, cultural, political, social and ecclesial context in which the textual objects of their study could play a transformative role. Of course, there is a need for expertise in specialized questions of textual history and philological detail, and there is a need for expertise in philosophical and literary developments which include but also transcend the framework of the study of the biblical texts. Not all Christian theology is biblical, but there ought not to be any Christian theology which is not at least properly informed about the biblical sources of Christian faith.

In view of these observations I would strongly suggest that we try to organize university positions and seminars in biblical theology and require from their occupants and participants a thorough knowledge of interpretative theory, theological method and the pluralism of biblical theologies as well as a readiness to transcend their confessional theological heritage and constraints. Such an establishment of an integrative yet open discipline in our faculties of theology would signal to students that Christian theology cannot do without a proper biblical-theological foundation. However, as long as we do not expect such an integrated knowledge and research orientation from ourselves as scholars we shall not be in a good position to convince our students of its need.

Conclusion: The Limits of Biblical Theology

I wish to conclude this paper by stressing the limits of such a project of a new biblical theology. Biblical theology as envisaged here has a distinct focus, namely the study of the reflection on God in the Hebrew scriptures and the New Testament. The emergence of monotheism in the social and religious context of ancient Israel; the prophetic critique of certain misconceptions of God; the liturgical, historical, liberationist, sapiential, and providential reflection on God in the Hebrew scriptures, and the diverse reflections on the experience of God in the ministry, passion and resurrection of Jesus of Nazareth in the texts of the New Testament should be studied with the help of the best hermeneutical strategies.

But the result of these interpretations must then be assessed in the wider context both of our contemporary search for adequate ways of understanding God and God's aims and plans with our universe, and of our effort to understand the theological concerns of our own post-biblical tradition as well as those of other religious traditions. Hence, biblical theology could function as one essential part of this much larger reflection on God.

In the light of contemporary hermeneutics and of feminist, political, liberationist, ecological, cosmological and philosophical critiques of Jewish and Christian traditions, it seems to me to be a promising enterprise to raise the question of God again today. Although thoroughly aware of the ideological baggage which this question carries, we may nevertheless be able to discuss the traces of God in our universe, and in this context to attend to the reflection on God by our biblical and post-biblical forbears. Instead of violating the texts once again by imposing on them well-known theological ideologies, we may be able now to reread these texts with a searching heart and mind. Instead of looking for proofs to suggest that our confessional ideologies and particular social concerns were always right, we may look again for the traces of God beyond these ideological obsessions. The unsatisfactory biblical theologies of the past do not excuse us from the task of cultivating a new sense for the development, continuities and discontinuities of the various strands of biblical reflection on God. Even the misuse of hermeneutics by theologians in the past does not offer sufficient reason to discourage biblical and theological interpreters of the Bible from developing common research projects on the only question which really seems to matter to most people, namely the question of ultimate meaning. Thirty centuries of patriarchal, confessional, authoritarian and other ideological domestication of references to God point indeed to a discouraging and terrible legacy. But then, there are the prophets old and new, there are the women and men who like Jesus have resisted religious tyranny and ideology and have searched for God's mysterious presence beyond the control of religious and atheistic systems. I am therefore convinced that a new, open, critical and self-critical reflection on this mystery will find much encouragement and orientation from an equally open, critical and self-critical theological reading of the Bible.

Notes

1. Karl Barth, *Der Römerbrief*, 2nd ed. (1922), Zurich: Theologischer Verlag 1978, xii.
2. Robert Morgan with John Barton, *Biblical Interpretation*, Oxford: Oxford University Press 1988, 179.
3. See in this context also Phyllis Trible's contribution to the present volume (pp. 32ff. above).
4. Rudolf Bultmann, 'Is Exegesis Without Presuppositions Possible?', in Kurt Mueller-Vollmer (ed.), *The Hermeneutics Reader: Texts of the German Tradition from the Enlightenment to the Present*, Oxford: Blackwell 1985, 242–55, here 242.
5. For a more detailed assessment of Bultmann's contribution to theological hermeneutics see my *Theological Hermeneutics: Development and Significance*, London: Macmillan 1991, 137–47.
6. Ernst Fuchs, 'The New Testament and the Hermeneutical Problem', in James M. Robinson and John B. Cobb, Jr (eds), *The New Hermeneutic*, New Frontiers in Theology 2, New York: Harper & Row 1964, 110–45; here 144.
7. Peter Stuhlmacher's hermeneutical vision also follows this model. See his *Vom Verstehen des Neuen Testaments: Eine Hermeneutik*, NTD Ergänzungsreihe 6, 2nd ed., Göttingen: Vandenhoeck & Ruprecht 1986, esp. 222–25.
8. Gerhard Ebeling, 'God and Word', in David E. Klemm, (ed.), *Hermeneutical Inquiry*, vol. 1.: *The Interpretation of Texts*, Atlanta: Scholars Press 1986, 195–224, here 212.
9. See Paul Ricoeur, *Hermeneutics and the Human Sciences*, ed. and trans. John B. Thompson, Cambridge, Cambridge University Press 1981, 63–100.

10. For a more detailed assessment of the interplay between reader and text in the act of reading see my *Text and Interpretation as Categories of Theological Thinking*, trans. Thomas J. Wilson, Dublin: Gill & Macmillan 1988, 104–19.

11. For a more detailed analysis of the contribution of text-linguistics to theological hermeneutics, see *Text and Interpretation as Categories of Theological Thinking*, 75–119.

12. Friedrich Schleiermacher, *Kurze Darstellung des theologischen Studiums zum Behuf einleitender Vorlesungen*, ed. Heinrich Scholz, Darmstadt: Wissenschaftliche Buchgesellschaft 1977.

5

Allegory and the Ethics of Reading

Frances Young

Modernism and the Demise of Allegory

There seems to be a fundamental distaste for, or even revulsion against, the whole business of allegory. Why is this? Basically, I think because we feel that there is something dishonest about allegory. If you interpret a text by allegorizing it, you seem to be saying that it means something which it patently does not. It is irrelevant, arbitrary: by allegory, it is said, you can make any text mean anything you like.

So Andrew Louth in a chapter entitled 'Return to Allegory'.[1] And we knew what he meant. We too had been brought up to distinguish between *exēgēsis* and *eisēgēsis*, and to accept the discipline of seeking the so-called original meaning. That almost instinctive sense that allegory was dishonest made it difficult to take Patristic exegesis seriously. Allegory was unethical.

It was also perceived to be unscriptural. The twentieth century had seen a radical reaction against the long-standing assumption that the parables were to be taken as allegories.[2] Jülicher had insisted that they had one point not many, turning them into simple moral sermon illustrations. Dodd and Jeremias had laboured to re-create their life-setting so as to demonstrate how they carried Jesus' message of the Kingdom. The parables were challenging and sharp vignettes, directed *ad hominem*, whose cutting edge had been for too long smoothed over by the mistakes of allegorical interpretation.

But there was another presupposition which strengthened those assumptions, namely the dogma our generation was brought up on that Christianity was a 'historical religion'. Against 'other-worldly' understandings of the Christian tradition, there had been a 'this-worldly' reaction, reinforced both by the so-called 'sense of history' as past and different which had emerged in the modern world, and by the apologetic need to defend the history of Christian origins against the charge that it was a myth or contained mythical elements. Allegory was inextricably mixed up with spiritual speculations rather than hard, defensible, historical facts. It was therefore more than dishonest, for in the modern context it was frankly useless – indeed an embarrassment.

The power of these assumptions can be seen in what now seem to me to be rather curious attempts to justify so-called traditional 'typology', and distinguish it from allegory. As Louth notes, the word 'typology' is a recent coinage. It has often been stressed that the writers of the early church use a variety of terms, *tropologia*, *allēgoria*, *anagōgia*, etc., which shade into one another and cannot be clearly distinguished; of these, 'typology' is not one, though there is much talk of *typoi*.

The modern distinction between typology and allegory was formally advanced by Lampe and Woollcombe.[3] Summarizing it in my own way, it went something like this: typology, unlike allegory, could be justified in the modern world because it represented a genuine historical perception, that sacred or revealing events have a family likeness, follow a pattern or type, simply because they are grounded in the consistency of God's providential love. So the typological parallel, much beloved of the early church, between Passover/Exodus and its fulfilment in Christ need not be jettisoned in essence, only the absurd allegorical details exploited to elaborate it. The authority of Daniélou[4] lay behind an essentially similar distinction between events and words, the first being associated with typology, the second with allegory. For Daniélou typology represented a kind of 'sacrament of the future'. The interest in eschatology undergirded a positive response to prefigurative events to which texts gave testimony, even if the notion of texts consisting of symbolic language, riddles to be unpacked by allegorical techniques, was unacceptable.

It all sounded so clear and convincing. There might be a resurgence of interest in Origen, but when it came to his biblical exegesis, it was so obviously a child of its time, fascinating but quite misguided. The title of R.P.C. Hanson's book, *Allegory and Event*,[5] speaks for itself.

Origen was really out of tune with the Bible, he argued, since he had no historical sense. The historical earthing of the biblical material and the historical nature of the Christian religion Hanson took for granted, an unquestioned dogma. So Origen's inability to grasp the importance of event and history for incarnation or Bible is judged unfavourably. Allegory, everyone assumed, permits escape from events and facts, not to mention the constraints of language, or the so-called 'original meaning'. Allegory must be false, deceptive, inappropriate as a method of exegesis.

Reaction against Modernist Historicism

But now the context has dramatically changed. The set of assumptions I have outlined has been challenged. It turns out that the books of scripture are not simply historical documents permitting access to revelatory events behind the text to which the texts give testimony. For it is only the way the story is told in the biblical material that makes the events significant in any sense. That means we are dealing with literature, and response to story, no matter how 'history-like', involves dimensions other than a documentary reading.

The demise of Biblical Theology signalled the coming challenge, and is well described and analysed in the writings of James Barr.[6] Following Maurice Wiles, Barr pointed out that it was by no means clear what it meant to claim that Christianity was a historical religion. In the claim a number of different elements were confused.[7] Different theological options relate to his six alternative meanings. I would add to his analysis the point that in the claim that Christianity is a historical religion, one may discern two distinct but intertwined characteristics of modern biblical scholarship: (1) defensiveness in the face of recognition that if certain events had not happened then Christian claims were vulnerable, giving rise to a strong element of apologetic in the attempt to claim historical factuality; and (2) enthusiasm for a salvation-historical approach which claimed to identify saving events discrete from yet enmeshed in the historical process, and believed to be the subject of the biblical witness. Both served the dogmatic concern to uphold the anti-docetic argument, a concern which the early church would have shared and most certainly endorsed, but without the same anxiety about historicity or 'event' in the modern sense.

Simply to state these confusions reveals the extent to which this historical emphasis was a novelty, recognizably culturally specific to the modern world. The principal aim was proof of a past revelation: whereas the concern and purpose of biblical narrative appears often to be less attesting past events, more throwing light on future meaning.[8] To treat the Bible as the Book of the Acts of God is not only fraught with philosophical difficulties, but fails to acknowledge the extent to which events become a story in which God participates by the way it is told. Coupled with increasing scepticism about the unity or continuity of Biblical Theology, the idea that revelation is not in the words of scripture but in events behind the text, events to which we only have access by reconstructing them from texts handled as historical documents, was increasingly challenged.

> Revelation through history was supposed to be characteristic of Hebrew thought ... [But] Israel's genius was never directed towards the interpretation of history ... In fact a historical mode of perception was never a primary mark of distinction between Israel and her neighbours ...[9]

Thus the claim that revelation in history is the distinctive characteristic of the Bible has begun to feel shaky, though the idea continues to have a long afterlife. The Bible tells a 'history-like' story, but historical categories do not exhaust the possibilities of biblical interpretation. The meaning of the Bible is not imprisoned in archaeology or past events, now almost inaccessible despite massive efforts at investigation and reconstruction.

Now if history, so important for modern readers for a variety of reasons, turns out not to have been so, or at least not in the same way, for ancient readers, clearly it may have been a modern projection to suppose that parable did not mean allegory, a view advanced despite the fact that allegory was acknowledged to be one among those elements covered by *māshāl*, and irrespective of the reality that allegorical reading was a widespread assumption for ancient readers. We shall have to return to close investigation of what exactly was meant by allegory, and whether all allegory is of a similar kind, but from a strictly historical perspective, John Drury was surely right to challenge the Dodd-Jeremias approach to parables in his essay on the origins of Mark's parables in *Ways of Reading the Bible*:[10]

The parables in Mark are, briefly and clumsily put, historical

106

allegories mixing concealment and revelation in the sort of riddling symbolism which is an ingredient of apocalyptic.

And that is what Drury successfully documents, beginning with the range of reference of the word *māshāl* in the Hebrew Bible, distinguishing, in particular, prophetic utterances of an allegorical kind like those in Ezekiel, riddles and fables, and showing how in apocalyptic, current historical situations were symbolically represented in allegorical form, deliberately obscure yet meant to be 'cracked', and revealing the secret mystery of the future. The modern anti-allegorical definition of parable distorts the text of Mark. In fact, if we are to understand how the biblical books were read by those readers for whom they were written, symbolism and allegory have to be taken into account – still more if we are to understand those who passed them down to us as a scriptural canon.

Finally, there has been the hermeneutical revolution. Andrew Louth's work with which we began drew upon the hermeneutics of Gadamer to challenge the idea that the meaning of texts is constituted by the original intention of the author. He drew in as ally the so-called New Criticism, and especially the views of T.S. Eliot: no explanation can exhaust the meaning of a poem, and an explanation of its meaning is not provided by a history of how it came to be written. Louth argues that like poetry, scripture is, as Newman put it, *mira profunditas*, a depth, a complexity, 'a richness derived from the mystery to which it is the introduction, of which it is the unfolding.' For Louth, Gadamer's observation that the 'infinite intermediary of tradition' lies between us and those who produced the classic texts of the past also encourages a reconsideration of the allegorical tradition which drew out different senses of scripture.

Within biblical studies itself, first structuralism, then literary critical methods of other kinds, not to mention the influence of Paul Ricoeur, has pressed upon us the sense that a text has a life of its own over which the original author has no control, nor is the author in any way privileged with respect to its interpretation. The writing-reading relation is not the same as the dialogical relation. These movements seem to permit the possibility that an author, especially a prophet, may have said more than he/she consciously knew. So the Bible must be regarded as a 'classic' with a plenitude of meaning, capable of transcending the immediate context from which its texts emerged. Its narratives reflect the fundamental structures of all narratives: its discrete texts acquire new meanings through constant adaptation and reinterpretation, by incorporation into a canon, and by a long tradition of interpretation. No longer could one justify the critical attempt to cut away all this to unearth the original form of the text and its original meaning.

Many have moved even further under the influence of recent literary theory: a text has no meaning in itself – it is merely a series of marks on a page – until a reader takes it up and begins to invest those symbols with meaning. The act of reading, rather than the act of authoring, is the crucial locus in which meaning is generated. Objectivity would therefore seem to be illusory, and *exēgēsis* essentially *eisēgēsis*. In principle there are many different readings of a text, and the ideological stance which the reader adopts will materially affect the way the text is read.

The whole course of biblical studies in the modern period is thus brought into question, challenged at a fundamental philosophical level. And even if we wanted one, there is no ultimate sanction against allegory. Readers are invited to read themselves into texts, and allegory might be regarded as one way of making a text mean something meaningful to the reader. There is no responsibility to the illusory 'original meaning' or to the absent author. There is therefore no dishonesty in allegory after all. Indeed, might it not be expedient to allegorize 'the Jews' in John's Gospel so as to appropriate a text whose destructive effects have become embarrassing in the post-holocaust world?

The Ethics of Reading

Such a question immediately alerts us to the difficulties with a radical postmodernist position. The fact is that these texts have fostered anti-Semitism, and it is too easy to pretend that they have no history or mean something other than the words they obviously contain. It is simply not possible to pretend that a text is a blank sheet of paper which we can read how we like. Our instinctive feeling is that how we read texts raises moral issues.

The question of the ethics of reception was first raised for me by George Steiner's book, *Real Presences*, and followed up by exploring Wayne Booth's *The Company We Keep – An Ethics of Fiction* and Werner Jeanrond's *Text and Interpretation as Categories of Theological Thinking*.[11] A word from each will set the direction of the discussion: 'No reading is ethically neutral, since every reading represents an answer to a textual claim, an answer which may be responsible or irresponsible' (Jeanrond, p. 128). '... [N]o serious writer, composer, painter has ever doubted ... that his work bears on good and evil ... A message is being sent; to a purpose' (Steiner, p. 145), and so the presence of the 'other' impinging on us requires our respect and attention, a certain tact, welcome, civility, courtesy. 'To begin with doubt is to destroy the datum' (Booth, p. 32); we read for improvement, and commonly experience being taken over by what we read – so that 'friendship' is the most appropriate metaphor of reading.

The burden of all three discussions is that text and reader interact. 'I serve myself best, as reader, when I both honour an author's offering for what it is, in its full "otherness" from me, and take an active critical stance against what seem to me its errors and excesses' (Booth, p. 135). Courtesy towards the text does not require capitulation, but a responsible reading articulates difference. It is not simply by identifying ourselves with characters in the story, or with the implied author, but by differentiation, whether by sympathetic listening across differences of culture and time, or by critical distancing, that we properly engage with what we read. Wayne Booth's ambiguous response to *Huckleberry Finn*, once the issue of racism was made overt, is not unlike the potentially ambiguous response of Christians to those texts of early Christianity which have fostered anti-Semitism. The actual reader, especially of a text from the past, is not identical with the reader implied by the text, and an ethical reading has to take account of that gap. But critical assessment cannot neutralize the challenge of a classic text to reshape the reader's world. A communication is to be received with respect and attention.

So to take the ethics of reading seriously would appear to reduce the extent to which readers can treat texts arbitrarily. To respect the 'otherness' of the text and to articulate difference would appear, in the case of texts from the distant past, to require some kind of reaffirmation of the importance of placing them in historical context, of recognizing that language is earthed in time, place and culture, and reading involves what the ancients would call *hermeneia* – translation and interpretation. Historical criticism may become subtly different in its character and goal in the context of post-modern pluralism, losing its apologetic interest in the events behind the text, but it must surely have a role in aiding the articulation of identities and differences, so facilitating an appropriately ethical reading. It is, I think, no accident that sociological readings have radicalized the sense of the incarnation of texts in social settings and therefore demanded new attempts to locate them historically, at the very time when hermeneutical theory has purported to loose them from their historical moorings.

Yet the imperialism of the old modernist claim to be able to state the original and therefore the right meaning of the text is clearly on the retreat on three grounds: (1) the fact that 'assured results' have largely proved so ephemeral and contentious; (2) the evident truth that, although some debates about meaning are soluble since language is in the public domain – indeed in some limited areas real progress has been made in New Testament exegesis – there is no end to the process of discussion, for language also enshrines infinite possibilities; (3) the kinds of hermeneutical considerations we have been taking account of, namely, the role of the reader in 'realizing' a text so as to participate in appropriate interaction with it.

So what about allegory? In the light of these remarks it would seem that respect for the text would rule out arbitrary *eisēgēsis*, and the allegorical readings of someone like Origen persistently provoke the suspicion of arbitrariness. Yet there are two reasons for hesitation before dismissing allegory. The first is a historical one, one we have already touched on, namely the prevalence of allegory as a strategy in ancient literature: to that justice must be done if we are to respect the 'otherness' of these texts. The other is our interest in participation in texts by readers, a process which inevitably involves a kind of allegory, a relationship of *mimēsis* (or imitation) as the reader is taken up into the text.[12] To proceed further we must clearly try to discover how allegory might be defined and what allegory has involved.

The Nature of Allegory

Once we set out on this exploration we soon find that allegory covers a multitude of things. Somehow, differentiation of types of allegory would seem to be vital if we are to assess what kinds of allegorical procedures might be drawn into an ethical reading of biblical texts.

I suggest that differentiating types of allegory is not a methodological issue: methods or techniques such as etymology, gematria and personification are particularly associated with allegory in almost all types, but are not themselves helpful for analysis. Rather, differentiation is a matter of context and strategy. Having disposed of the mirage of typology,[13] I propose the following seven categories of allegory, though one shades into another. Some are especially characteristic of certain Hellenistic movements, but others are ancient and universal, biblical and rabbinic as well as Hellenic:

1. Rhetorical allegory, where allegory is adopted as a figure of speech on a spectrum with irony and metaphor.
2. Parabolic allegory, of a kind found in fables and riddles.
3. Prophetic allegory, hidden and riddling revelation found in oracles, dreams, symbolic visions, or narrative signs.
4. Moral allegory, where the moral of a text is sought for paedeutic or paraenetic reasons, e.g. by particulars being universalized as examples.
5. Natural or psychological allegory, where a mythological text is read as referring to forces interacting in the world according to accepted scientific norms.
6. Philosophical allegory, where the transcendent world is revealed, in veiled fashion, through the material world, and/or a text employing earthly language to convey heavenly meanings.
7. Theological allegory, whereby Christ, or the creative and saving purposes of the Trinity, becomes the true meaning of life, the universe, the text and everything.

What follows does not attempt to illustrate or discuss these types – a task beyond the scope of this paper – but offers some complementary discussion of the allegorical process as it took place in a world where it was less alien than it appears to us.

The word *allēgoria* is derived from a Greek verb meaning 'to speak in public' compounded with the adjective *allos* meaning 'other'.[14] Ancient definitions all ring the changes on the same theme: allegory is 'to mean something other than what one says'. It is distinguished in textbooks on style as a *tropē*, a 'turn' or figure of speech, and lies on a spectrum with metaphor and irony. By the time of Quintillian it was recognized that a continuous metaphor makes an allegory, and personification, e.g. of abstract qualities, became an increasingly common feature of the compositional allegory. In the rhetorical tradition, therefore, it might refer to deliberate obfuscation on the part of the author, implying the adoption of guarded or elite language, things only to be said in secret or unworthy of the crowd: it was at the very least a sophisticated conceit. In apocalyptic, as Drury has shown us, it produced a riddle to be cracked.

One fundamental distinction to be explored is the difference between such compositional allegory and allegorical interpretation.[15] It is one thing, one might think, for an author to adopt a particular figure of speech and develop it, and then for the reader to identify this process in exegetical analysis; it is another thing for a reader or interpreter to suggest that a whole text has an 'undersense' or *hyponoia*, and should not be read according to what might be claimed to be its 'obvious' meaning.

But there are reasons for suspecting that the distinction cannot hold for too long: (1) the weight this puts on authorial intention and the difficulty, in some cases, of identifying the 'plain sense' – a feature of postmodern sensibility in relation to texts; (2) the ancient propensity to attribute meaning to dreams and what we might call unauthored phenomena; (3) the fact that those who engaged in allegorical interpretation certainly thought that the *hyponoia* was what the author intended. Stoics thought that the original philosophical wisdom was known to Homer, and he really meant what they thought he meant. Origen believed that the Holy Spirit had clothed the divine *skopos* (aim or intent) in the dress of the wording, and only those who probed for the deeper meaning understood what the text was about. It was a commonplace in rhetorical education to distinguish between the subject-matter and the style, and the good author was the one who chose the proper stylistic dress in which to clothe his argument. The aim of the author was to convince the hearer. The conceit of allegory would challenge the hearers and divide them into those who saw through it and those who did not. For Origen, the Word of God performs likewise.

So, to progress we should shift the focus from the intention of the author to the response of the reader to the text, and enquire in what sense the reader submitted to constraints in interpretation. The educational process in grammatical and rhetorical schools was learning first to 'realize' the classics by reading them with understanding, then to emulate them in one's own compositions. Identifying figures of speech, recognizing the multivalent creativity of poetic language, was part of that basic educational process. Not only does allegory lie on a spectrum, and cannot be sharply differentiated from other figures of speech, but there is allegory and allegory.

Jon Whitman[16] helps us to grasp the dynamics of allegory:

> ... Our language is constantly telling us that something is what it is not....

> All fiction ... tries to express a truth by departing from it in some way. It may embellish its subject, rearrange it, or simply verbalize it, but in every case, that ancient dislocation of words from their objects will keep the language at one remove from what it claims to present. Allegory is the extreme case of this divergence ... In its obliquity, allegorical writing thus exposes in an extreme way the foundation of fiction in general.

> The more allegory exploits the divergence between corresponding levels of meaning, the less tenable the correspondence becomes. Alternatively, the more it closes ranks and emphasizes the correspondence, the less oblique and therefore the less allegorical, the divergence becomes.

Taking up this perspective, my suggestion would be that the crucial differences between forms of allegorical reading lie in the way in which the correspondences and divergences are conceived.

In analysing forms of speech, it was generally assumed in ancient schools that the author had chosen the linguistic devices employed for a specific rhetorical purpose to do with the intended effect on the audience, though the particular aim might vary within a given work. The text provided clues. It also provided constraints. And it was in this area of clues and constraints that we find the source of different readings, and the underlying issues in debates about language and about allegory in the ancient world. One of our constant perplexities is how to interpret the procedures of an Irenaeus who attacks gnostic allegory, and from our perspective allegorizes himself, or how to characterize the Antiochene reaction against allegory when their own exegetical practice indulges in moral and dogmatic readings of a kind we find difficult to accommodate in the sort of literal and historical readings modernity has approvingly projected on to them. In both cases, the answer seems to lie in the perception of how surface-text and deeper meaning are related – indeed we can see in the debate about allegory in the early church a reflection of debates about language in the ancient intellectual scene.

There were two theories of language discussed in the ancient world: the *physis* (= nature) theory and the *thesis* (= convention) theory. Etymology originated in the first view that there was a natural connection between language and reality, at least of a mimetic kind. So names were more than signifiers – they pointed to significance. Others took the second view, regarding language as a matter of convention, thus accounting for differences between languages. Theophilus of Antioch, interestingly, believed in a pristine natural language which was corrupted and fragmented at Babel – thereafer *thesis* reigned! If conventional signs might become tokens or symbols, natural names would in some sense mimetically image the reality they represented. Thus whatever the theory of language, it was assumed that language represents, or refers to, a reality other than itself, the debate being about the precise relationship between the reality and the linguistic representation.

It is this kind of distinction with respect to language that gives us a clue to different perceptions of how a text might represent or refer to something other than itself. *Mimēsis* (representation) may occur through genuine likeness or analogy, an 'ikon' or image, or it may occur by a symbol, something unlike which stands for the reality. The 'ikon' will resemble what it represents, but symbols are not representations in that sense, having a much more complex relationship with reality as mere 'tokens' whose analogous relationship with what is symbolized is less clear.[17] Ikonic allegory would find a higher degree of correspondence between the various features of the text, the passage or narrative as a whole reflecting or mirroring in the narrative structure the 'undersense' adduced. Symbolic exegesis would tend to focus on particular verbal 'tokens' which consistently signify specific heavenly realities in the scriptures taken as a whole, but at the level of particular passages may produce a more piecemeal and apparently arbitrary meaning.

So, recently[18] I have distinguished three exegetical strategies in the patristic material which might be described as allegorical: the mimetic, the ikonic and the symbolic. In the ancient world, the 'mimetic' nature of all language and literature was taken for granted. Because art imitated life, it had moral value as exemplary or as a dire warning. Plutarch urges the appropriate techniques for ensuring that literature provides a moral paedeutic, with the critique of Plato and other philosophers much in mind. In a similar way, early Christian paraenetic exploited the exemplary value of stories and characters in a new alien body of literature, the Bible. Another mimetic feature found in scripture arose from its assumed prophetic or oracular character: narratives provided 'types' or patterns of things to come, and so the significance of current events or the outline of future possibilities could be discerned in the 'shadow' found in the biblical material, e.g. the outstretched arms of Moses ensuring victory over the Amalekites prefiguring the cross. It is, of course, this feature which has been utilized in characterizing so-called 'typology', but this example shows that it is the mimetic stamp (*typos*) in the description of Moses' action which is more significant than the 'event'.

Such *mimēsis* contributed to the reading of a text as speaking of some referent other than that which it purported to describe, as did the 'grammatical' procedure of identifying etymologies and metaphors, for both gave linguistic grounds for supposing that deeper or less than straightforward meanings were present. All this was common ground for the ancient reader, and facilitated allegory.

Someone like Origen was a philologist.[19] More than is generally realized he paid attention to the letter or wording of the text, using all the techniques of the grammarian. In the letter, however, he found certain stumbling-blocks, and these he took as textual clues to the fact that the true meaning lay elsewhere. The letter of the text was a collection of conventional signs or symbols. He found the coherence of scripture in its reference to fall and redemption, to the divine purpose in creation and revelation, in the spiritual journey back home, in the communication of God's true Word, everything pointing to Christ. This was the Spirit's *skopos*, and everything related to this divine *paedeusis*. The wording of the text was both vehicle and veil. Names and numbers were symbols, and the correspondence between words and subjects gave access to a narrative or meaning divergent from the earthly story which was nevertheless its vehicle.

But for Origen as for Irenaeus, there were constraints. The overarching story enshrined in the Rule of Faith provided the framework, the core of revelation to which scripture universally testified. The problem with gnostic allegory was that the wording was rearranged to produce a different *hypothesis*. Irenaeus accused gnostics of creating a *cento* of scripture, a *cento* being a new composition built out of lines or half-lines cribbed from Homer or Vergil; as Irenaeus put it, someone who knew Homer would recognize Homer's words but not Homer's *hypothesis*.

Those who reacted against Origen, namely the Antiochenes,[20] were no less sure that scripture pointed to moral and spiritual truths, but they found such truths imaged in the narrative coherence of the text, rather than lying outside the text and merely symbolized in what seemed a set of arbitrary correspondences. Thus a text offered internal clues to its ikonic intention, whereas the clues to symbolic language lay for Origen in the stumbling-blocks and impossibilities for taking it at its face-value.

Challenging the term allegory, they chose *theōria*, asserting that the allegorist abused Paul's term in Galatians 4.24, treating it as a blank authorization to abolish all meanings of divine scripture. Their understanding of the constraints was different. The story mattered, even if deeper significance lay in its features: Jesus used the boy's loaves and fish rather than creating out of nothing in order to stop the mouths of docetic heretics. So as Heraclitus in his *Homeric Allegories* sought a mirroring of natural and psychological forces in the narrative structure of the *Iliad*, so the Antiochenes sought a mirroring of moral and spiritual truth in the coherence of narratives and the straightforward connections in the text. I have deliberately avoided using the word 'literal', because they certainly did not produce what we would call 'literal' interpretations, and they knew like everyone else that 'the letter' might be quite misleading since texts contain figures of speech like metaphor and irony. Their *theōria* like Origen's allegory was intended to probe for deeper meanings, but without destroying the coherence of the text's surface, whereas in their view Origen's allegory led to piecemeal and dis-integrative readings.

Allegory and the Ethics of Reading

This survey has given us some sense of the extent to which allegory is on a spectrum and hard to distinguish from other readings which assume the possibility of linguistic multivalence, but it also reveals that any reading which seeks a hermeneutic is bound to have features in common with allegory. In fact, the most recent study of allegory by David Dawson[21] is an attempt to show that allegorical reading is an important contributor to cultural revision. Allegory essentially says, 'You have read the text this way, but it should be read like this.' To that extent the development of ideological readings, like liberation theology or feminist theology, are forms of allegory. Even the once dominant historico-critical reading, against which such readings have reacted, may be regarded as in some sense allegorical in that it enabled the domestication of ancient texts to modern apologetic needs. It said, 'You used to read these texts as being obviously about dogma, but really they are about something else.' Every critical reading shares something with allegory; every attempt at entering the world of the text, or seeing the text as mirroring our world and reflecting it back to us, involves some degree of allegory.

And the supposed repudiation of allegory has been a dramatic loss to the Christian tradition. Andrew Louth, with whom we began, attempted to reclaim the traditional allegory of the church, drawing particularly on de Lubac's exposition in *Exégèse Mediévale*. For this tradition, Louth argued, symbolism enabled participation in the mystery of Christ, and it was in the liturgy that allegory came into its own. This was not the arbitrary *allēgoria verbi*, or what I have called symbolic allegory, but rather *allēgoria facti*. Louth explores an example, tracing the ways in which allegory opened up the theological significance of the story of the baptism of Christ, drawing the participant into response, 'a response of innocence and a soaring desire for God' like that of the dove. Allusion to the story of Noah draws in further correspondences to show that the storm is over, there is release from evil and peace with God. Allegory lets the echoes be heard, and so invites the hearer into the story of redemption.

I am increasingly sure that the modernist concern with historicity has cut us off from a living tradition of complex multivalent images which have resonated in Christian art and poetry as well as liturgy. The renewed interest in metaphor, in intertextual association, in spirituality, should, I suggest, open our eyes once more to the creative potential of at least mimetic and ikonic readings. Perhaps we may still feel some reservations about the symbolic allegory that seemed to encourage piecemeal reading, but recent work on both Origen and Didymus suggests that their procedures have not as yet been properly understood; and in any case I would not like to be heard pleading for their results, so much as for recognition that we need to become self-conscious of our own actual and potential allegorical reading. For some kind of allegory is involved in any hermeneutic, and the curious Two-Nature or sacramental possibilities that emerge from treating the biblical texts as Word of God seem to me to have been submerged by most modern readings.[22]

And so there are three reasons why an allegorical reading might also be an ethical reading:

1. It enables the reader to grapple constructively with the dynamic between divergences and connections, differences and similarities, as the reader allows the text to impinge on the self and/or the world of the present. It becomes unethical if it simply permits domestication of the text to the reader's perspectives so that the text merely reinforces identities already achieved or authorizes positions already held. But if it allows the right kind of engagement and response, it has potential for creative cultural challenge.

2. It enables associative links of poetic images, symbolic actions, parables, metaphors, stories, to be discerned, so that the rich inter-textuality of the Bible can be reclaimed. It becomes unethical if it spawns a gnostic loss of the biblical hypothesis. But whether the associations were consciously or unconsciously intended by the earthly authors of these texts, the potential of the linguistic realities was surely better reflected in traditional moral and spiritual exegesis which exploited such allegorical associations than it has ever been in the era of historical and documentary reading. Such reading is ethical precisely because it does better justice to the qualities of the texts themselves and the cultures from which they came.

3. Allegory self-consciously makes play with the inadequacies of human language for expressing the divine. Apophatic theology and allegory go together. Positivist views of language have impoverished theological reading of the Bible by reducing God to an item in the world of the biblical text. Allegorical reading can set free the soul for creative engagement with transcendence, and such spiritual reading with a certain open-endedness can alone do justice to the textual claim which the Bible makes, and so provide a truly ethical reading.

Postscript: this has been a ground-clearing exercise, and does not yet claim to have reached the stage of proposals for criteria or con-straints appropriate to a modern allegorical reading.

Notes

1. Andrew Louth, *Discerning the Mystery*, Oxford: Oxford University Press 1983.
2. The classic studies following Jülicher, *Die Gleichnisreden Jesu* (1899–

1910), are C.H. Dodd. *The Parables of the Kingdom*, London: Collins 1934. and J. Jeremias, *The Parables of Jesus*, ET London: SCM Press 1954.

3. G.W.H. Lampe and K.J. Woollcombe, *Essays in Typology*, London: SCM Press 1957.

4. Louth, op. cit., 118; cf. J. Daniélou, *From Shadows to Reality*, ET London: Burns & Oates 1960.

5. R.P.C. Hanson, *Allegory and Event*, London: SCM Press 1959.

6. James Barr, *The Bible in the Modern World*, London: SCM Press 1973, and the essays reprinted in *Explorations in Theology 7*, London: SCM Press 1980; cf. Maurice Wiles, 'In what sense is Christianity a "Historical Religion"?', in *Explorations in Theology 4*, London: SCM Press 1989.

7. Barr (*Explorations*, 31) suggests at least the following list: it meant that the 'historical course Christianity has followed is thereby right and normative'; or that 'because the religion is a historical one, its documents must be subject to the same kind of historical scrutiny as those of any other ideology'; or that 'the historical assertions made in its documents must be considered as historically accurate'; or that Christianity is not a system of timeless truths but a movement with a past and a future, only understood if you have a historical sense and explore its theology historically; or it implies existentialist encounter in historical existence; or that Christianity must be 'made to rest on that limited element in the sources which can stand as historically probable or reliable.' Elsewhere in his writings he examines the features of modern biblical scholarship which I highlight in the following sentences.

8. A point stressed by Barr, *Explorations*, 36.

9. *Explorations*, 37.

10. *Ways of Reading the Bible*, ed. Michael Wadsworth, Brighton: Harvester 1981.

11. George Steiner, *Real Presences*, London: Faber & Faber 1989: Wayne Booth, *The Company We Keep – An Ethics of Fiction*, California: University of California Press 1988: Werner Jeanrond, *Text and Interpretation as Categories of Theological thinking*, ET Dublin: Gill & Macmillan 1988. See further my paper, 'The Pastorals Epistles and the Ethics of Reception,' *JSNT* 45 (1992), 105–20.

12. See further my discussion in *The Art of Performance – towards a theology of Holy Scripture*, London: Darton, Longman & Todd 1990, chapter 7.

13. This matter was more fully discussed in my recent series of Speaker's Lectures in Oxford; the second series will be completed in 1993, and then hopefully publication will follow.

14. For the points in this paragraph I am particularly indebted to Jon

Whitman, *Allegory: the dynamics of an ancient and mediaeval technique*, Oxford: Oxford University Press 1987, Appendix I.

15. See Whitman, op. cit.
16. Ibid., 1–2.
17. For this distinction see James A. Coulter, *The Literary Microcosm: Theories of Interpretation in the Later Neoplatonists*, Leiden: Brill 1976.
18. Cf. note 13.
19. Cf. note 13. I understand my own discussion has been anticipated by Bernhard Neuschafer, *Origenes als Philologe*, Basle 1987, but I have not yet obtained this work.
20. See further my paper, 'The Rhetorical Schools and their influence on Patristic Exegesis', in the Chadwick Festschrift, *The Making of Orthodoxy*, ed. Rowan Williams, Cambridge: Cambridge University Press 1989, 182–199.
21. David Dawson, *Allegorical Readers and Cultural Revision in Ancient Alexandria*, California: University of California Press 1992.
22. See further, *The Art of Performance*.

6

God's Own (Pri)son: The Disciplinary Technology of the Cross

Stephen D. Moore

My father was a butcher. As a child, the inner geographical boundaries of my world extended from the massive granite bulk of the Redemptorist church squatting at one end of our street to the butcher's shop guarding the other end. Redemption, expiation, sacrifice, slaughter ... There was no city abattoir in Limerick in those days; each butcher did his own slaughtering. I recall the hooks, the knives, the cleavers; the terror in the eyes of the victim; my own fear that I was afraid to show; the crude stun-gun slick with grease; the stunned victim collapsing to its knees; the slitting of the throat; the filling of the basins with blood; the skinning and evisceration of the corpse; the wooden barrels overflowing with entrails; the crimson floor littered with hooves.

I also recall a Good Friday sermon by a Redemptorist preacher that recounted at remarkable length the atrocious agony felt by our sensitive Saviour as the nails were driven through his hands and feet. Strange to say, it was this recital, and not the other spectacle, that finally caused me to faint. Helped outside by my father, I vomited gratefully on the steps of the church.

'The Utterly Vile Death of the Cross'

The central symbol of Christianity is the figure of a tortured man. Attending an exhibition of instruments of torture in Rome, Page duBois reports: 'I gazed uneasily at the others visiting this spot ... I tried to imagine what brought them there. Was it a historical

121

curiosity about the Middle Ages, or the same desire that brings people to horror movies, or sexual desire invested in bondage and discipline? I was there too.'[1] Such unease would be almost unimaginable in a Sunday service, and yet the central spectacle is not altogether dissimilar. The Gospels may have contributed to the profound equanimity with which the average Christian views this grisly spectacle; 'they crucified him' is the extraordinarily restrained testimony of the evangelists (Mark 15.24; Matt. 27.35; Luke 23.33; John 19.18). Martin Hengel has written what amounts to a book-length elaboration of this stark statement.[2]

The burden of Hengel's *Crucifixion* is to show, through extensive appeal to ancient sources, why crucifixion was regarded as the most horrific form of punishment in the ancient world.[3] Far from being a dispassionate execution of justice, 'crucifixion satisfied the primitive lust for revenge and the sadistic cruelty of individual rulers and of the masses'.[4]

Even in the Roman empire, where there might be said to be some kind of 'norm' for the course of the execution (it included a flogging beforehand, and the victim often carried the beam to the place of execution, where he was nailed to it with outstretched arms, raised up and seated on a small wooden peg), the form of execution could vary considerably: crucifixion was a punishment in which the caprice and sadism of the executioners were given full rein. All attempts to give a perfect description of *the* crucifixion in archaeological terms are therefore in vain; there were too many different possibilities for the executioner.[5]

The implication, of course, is that the bald statement, 'they crucified [Jesus]', may still retain some of its secrets even when the historians and archaeologists are through interrogating it. In a chapter unambiguously titled, 'Crucifixion as a "Barbaric" Form of Execution of Utmost Cruelty', Hengel documents some of the possibilities open to the executioner.

Spectacle and Surveillance

... the crowds who had gathered there for the spectacle ...

Luke 23.48

Seventeen-hundred years later we find the executioners exploring other possibilities. Michel Foucault's *Discipline and Punish* opens with the following scene:

122

On 2 March 1757 Damiens the regicide was condemned 'to make the *amende honorable* before the main door of the Church of Paris', where he was to be 'taken and conveyed in a cart, wearing nothing but a shirt, holding a torch of burning wax weighing two pounds'; then, 'in the said cart, to the Place de Grève, where, on a scaffold that will be erected there, the flesh will be torn from his breasts, arms, thighs and calves with red-hot pincers, his right hand, holding the knife with which he committed the said parricide, burnt with sulphur, and, on those places where the flesh will be torn away, poured molten lead, boiling oil, burning resin, wax and sulphur melted together and then his body drawn and quartered by four horses and his limbs and body consumed by fire, reduced to ashes and his ashes thrown to the winds'.[6]

According to witnesses, the execution was badly botched; the quartering went on interminably, two more horses had to be brought in, 'and when that did not suffice, they were forced, in order to cut off the wretch's thighs, to sever the sinews and hack at the joints ...'.[7] The victim, meanwhile, forgave his executioners, Jesus-like, and begged them not to swear as they struggled to dismember him.

In time, as Foucault reports, the ritual of public torture became intolerable. 'Protests against the public executions proliferated in the second half of the eighteenth century: among the philosophers and theoreticians of the law; among lawyers and *parlementaires*; in popular petitions and among the legislators of the assemblies.'[8] The more spectacular forms of public execution gradually ceased, and judicial punishment was reestablished on a more 'humane' foundation. 'In the worst of murderers, there is one thing, at least, to be respected when one punishes: his "humanity". The day was to come, in the nineteenth century, when this "man", discovered in the criminal, would become the target of penal intervention, the object that it claimed to correct and transform, the domain of a whole series of "criminological" sciences ...'[9] No longer could judicial punishment be justified as the rightful vengeance of a sovereign on a rebellious subject.

A giant step forward in the history of judicial practice? Foucault does not think so, which is what makes *Discipline and Punish* remarkable. For Foucault, the feudal 'society of the spectacle' was succeeded in the modern period by something altogether more sinister. The fearful spectacle of brutal punishment being publicly exacted on the body of a condemned criminal had at least the advantage of being open and direct. The degree of covert control over the individual that modern 'disciplinary societies' aspire to would have been unimaginable under the old regimes. In particular, for Foucault, the prison reforms of the nineteenth century concealed an iron fist of totalitarianism in a velvet glove of humanitarianism. 'In the totally ordered, hierocratized space of the nineteenth-century prison, the prisoner is put under constant surveillance, discipline, and education in order to transform him into what power as now organized in society demands that everyone become: docile, productive, hard-working, self-regulating, conscience-ridden, in a word, "normal" in every way.'[10]

In a 1978 interview Foucault remarked: 'I'm delighted that historians found no major error in [*Discipline and Punish*] and that, at the same time, prisoners read it in their cells.'[11] Recently, however, Page duBois has questioned the story that *Discipline and Punish* tells. She notes that the tripartite structure of the book shows 'Torture' (the subject matter of Part One) yielding first to 'Punishment' (Part Two) and then to 'Discipline' (Part Three), the implication being that state-sanctioned atrocities such as the execution by torture of transgressors have now receded into history, 'that we are all so thoroughly disciplined now, have so deeply internalized our own policing, that we no longer need the spectacle of punishment'.[12] Foucault states confidently: 'We are now far away from the country of tortures, dotted with wheels, gibbets, gallows, pillories.'[13] 'Tell it to the El Salvadorans', replies duBois.[14] In other words, the narrative of *Discipline and Punish* 'is resolutely Eurocentric'. Foucault's 'description of the transition from spectacular torture and execution to internalized discipline remains a local analysis'.[15] His narrative is further undermined by the fact that whereas state-sanctioned torture does indeed seem to be the exception rather than the rule today in Western Europe and North America, the substantial role that certain Western democracies have played in supporting regimes that routinely employ torture to enforce public order suggests a disturbing, symbiotic relationship between the 'societies of the spectacle' and the 'disciplinary societies', one that the seductive chronology of *Discipline and Punish* obscures.[16] These are serious criticisms. At the very least, they caution us that if we are to use *Discipline and Punish* as an analogical tool for a reconsideration of the relationship between violent punishment and internalized self-policing in the

New Testament (I shall be confining myself to the letters of Paul), we must allow for the possibility that the relationship may be symbiotic or parasitic.

'His Mighty and Annihilating Reaction'

Let us begin with Hengel's conclusion, which is that 'the earliest Christian message of the crucified messiah demonstrated the "solidarity" of the love of God with the unspeakable suffering of those who were tortured and put to death by human cruelty ...'[17] This is a moving interpretation of the crucifixion. It is complicated by a troubling question, however, one that Hengel can ill-afford to raise, having already argued that crucifixion 'is a manifestation of trans-subjective evil, a form of execution which manifests the demonic character of human cruelty and bestiality'.[18] The question is a simple one: Who inflicted the punishment of crucifixion on Jesus? Was it the procurator of Judaea, acting on behalf of the Roman Emperor? Or was it an even higher power, acting through the Roman authorities (cf. John 19.11; Acts 4.27–28; Rom. 13.1; I Cor. 2.8)?[19]

To interpret Jesus' death as punishment is to move within the ambit of the doctrine of atonement. Although it had a rich patristic history,[20] the doctrine came fully into its own only with St Anselm's *Cur Deus Homo*? (1097–98), where it was formulated as a 'theory of satisfaction'. The Anselmian form of the doctrine has generally been accepted by Roman Catholic theologians since the Middle Ages.[21] Moreover, as Gustaf Aulén notes, it has long been argued 'that a continuous line may be traced from Anselm, through medieval scholasticism, and through the Reformation, to the Protestant "Orthodoxy" of the seventeenth century'.[22] This is not to say, continues Aulén, that Anselm's teaching was merely regurgitated by his successors, 'for differences of view are noted in Thomas Aquinas and in the Nominalists, and the post-Reformation statements of the doctrine have a character of their own; nevertheless, there is a continuity of tradition, and the basis of it is that which Anselm laid'.[23] What Anselm laid can be paraphrased as follows:

> Sin is an offence against the majesty of God. In spite of his goodness, God cannot pardon sin without compounding with honor and justice. On the other hand, he cannot revenge himself on man for his offended honor; for sin is an offence of infinite

degree, and therefore demands infinite satisfaction; which means that he must either destroy humanity or inflict upon it the eternal punishments of hell. ... There is but one way for God to escape this dilemma without affecting his honor, and that is to arrange for some kind of *satisfaction*. He must have infinite satisfaction because the offense is immeasurable. ... Hence, the necessity of the *incarnation*. God becomes man in Christ; Christ suffers and dies in our stead....[24]

It is, of course, no coincidence that Anselm's interpretation of the crucifixion bears a striking resemblance to the feudal conception of judicial punishment as outlined in the opening chapters of *Discipline and Punish*. Under the feudal regime, 'the law ... represented the will of the sovereign; he who violated it must answer to the wrath of the king ... Thus, the power and integrity of the law were reasserted; the affront was righted. This excessive power found its form in the ritual of atrocity.'[25] The term 'ritual' is highly appropriate here. 'Under this type of regime the notion of crime is still not fully distinguished from that of sacrilege, so that punishment takes the form of a ritual intended not to "reform" the offender but to express and restore the sanctity of the law which has been broken.'[26]

The language of wrath and punishment applied to the crucifixion is by no means extinct even among critical exegetes. In his massive commentary on Romans, Douglas Moo has recently defended the traditional attribution to Paul of a doctrine of divine wrath and retribution, while attacking the revisionist school of thought that would reject or qualify this attribution.[27] Moo quotes approvingly Anders Nygren's paraphrase of Romans 1.18: 'As long as God is God, He cannot behold with indifference that His creation is destroyed and His holy will trodden underfoot. Therefore He meets sin with his mighty and annihilating reaction.'[28] Here we are not far from the world of Anselm, whatever about the world of Paul. We can almost hear the bones cracking on the wheel as the might of the offended sovereign bears down upon the body of the condemned.

'What a Primitive Mythology'

Not surprisingly, the doctrine of atonement has been an acute embarrassment for many other twentieth-century exegetes. Rudolf Bultmann is exemplary in this regard.[29] Traditionally the doctrine has been laid squarely at the feet of Paul. For Bultmann, as for the majority of critical scholars, Paul does not altogether deserve this dubious honour.[30] Paul's thought regarding sin contains two distinct strands, according to Bultmann, and these strands 'are not harmonized with each other'.[31] Most significant for us is the strand that Bultmann regards as least important. He concedes that there is in Paul a 'juristic conception of death as the punishment for sin'.[32] This Paul inherited from the 'Old Testament-Jewish tradition'.[33]

> *Death is the punishment for the sin a man has committed*; sinners are 'worthy of death' (Rom. 1.32 KJ), they have 'earned' death. So Paul can also say that ... the sinner by his death pays his debt, atones for his sin (Rom. 6.7). In such statements, death, we must recognize, is first thought of as the death which is natural dying, as Rom. 5.12ff. shows, according to which death as the punishment for sin was brought into the world by Adam's sin. Nevertheless, they also presuppose that this death will be confirmed – made final, so to say – by the verdict condemning them to 'destruction' which God will pronounce over sinners on the judgment day (Rom. 2.6–11).[34]

Faced with this prospect, the sinner is in urgent need of justification through the blood of Jesus, 'a propitiatory sacrifice by which forgiveness of sins is brought about; which is to say: by which the guilt contracted by sins is cancelled'.[35] Closely bound up with the idea of propitiatory sacrifice, moreover, is the idea of vicarious sacrifice, 'which likewise has its origin in the field of cultic-juristic thinking'.[36] 'The same phrase (*hyper hēmōn*) that is translated "for us" can also express this idea, meaning now: "instead of us", "in place of us".'[37] Bultmann detects a vicarious theology in Gal. 3.13 ('becoming a curse in our stead') and II Cor. 5.21 ('he made him who was unacquainted with sin to be sin in our stead'; cf. Rom. 8.3). He argues that both ideas, vicarious and propitiatory sacrifice, merge in II Cor. 5.14ff.[38]

Bultmann himself has little time for such ideas. 'How can the guilt of one man be expiated by the death of another who is sinless – if indeed one may speak of a sinless man at all?' he asks in some exasperation in 'New Testament and Mythology'. 'What primitive notions of guilt and righteousness does this imply? And what primitive idea of God? ... What a primitive mythology it is, that a divine Being should ... atone for the sins of men through his own blood!'[39] The sacrificial hypothesis entails a *sacrificium intellectus* that Bultmann is determined to avoid.

In his *Theology of the New Testament*, therefore, Bultmann is careful to highlight those passages in which Paul appears to interpret Jesus' crucifixion as potential deliverance from the *power of sin*, and to gloss over passages in which Paul appears to interpret the crucifixion as sacrificial atonement for *actual sins*. The latter passages do 'not contain Paul's characteristic view'.[40] For Paul, 'Christ's death is not merely a sacrifice which cancels the guilt of sin (i.e., the punishment contracted by sinning), but is also *the means of release from the powers of this age: Law, Sin, and Death*.'[41] Like the judicial reformers of the eighteenth century, then, Bultmann finds the idea of a vengeful sovereign, one capable of inflicting brutal physical punishment on his rebellious subjects, to be intolerable. Such primitive ideas 'make the Christian faith unintelligible and unacceptable to the modern world'.[42]

'Once you suppress the idea of vengeance,' writes Madan Sarup, 'punishment can only have a meaning within a technology of reform'[43] – or a *theology* of reform, as here. The doctrine of atonement, in its classic mediaeval form, amounts to an interpretation of Jesus' death as public execution by torture for transgression, the righting of an affront to the sovereign power – the injured party not being the Roman Emperor, however (as those who administer the punishment unwittingly suppose), but the Divine Majesty Himself. Uncomfortable with such primitive notions, Bultmann prefers to attribute to Paul – the 'real' Paul – an interpretation of Jesus' death as a potential *reform*, an unique opportunity for the transgressor to be utterly transformed from within.[44] The event of the cross promises freedom from sin. 'But this freedom is not a static quality: it is freedom *to obey*. The indicative implies an imperative.'[45] A horrific act of violence, then, execution by public torture, gives birth to an altogether different order in which obedient action springs spontaneously from within and no longer from any external coercion. This is also the transition that *Discipline and Punish* describes.

Howard Eilberg-Schwartz, introducing *The Savage in Judaism*, remarks: 'the work of deconstructive critics ... and Foucault ... has taught me that the key to a tradition often lies in what it excludes.'[46] Can it be that the key to the Pauline interpretation of Jesus' crucifixion, as reconstructed by scholars such as Bultmann, lies in what that reconstruction excludes or plays down, namely, the 'Jewish

sacrificial' element in Paul's thought? At least since the Enlightenment, Christian theology and philosophy has tended to regard
certain aspects of ancient Jewish religion as 'savage' (whether or not
that word is used), as Eilberg-Schwartz has shown.[47] The practice of
sacrifice in particular has caused Christian apologists much discom-
fort. 'On the one hand, this practice certainly appears barbaric and
crude and has parallels in the practices of savages. On the other
hand, the Christian revelation [as commonly interpreted] is itself
premised on the idea that God sacrificed a son as expiation for the
world.'[48] What precisely is it about this premise that tends to make
critical exegetes uncomfortable? Bultmann has already directed us to
the answer. A glance at Léon-Dufour's *Life and Death in the New
Testament* will help us to see it more clearly.

Léon-Dufour's monograph returns repeatedly to the motifs of
sacrifice, expiation, and atonement. For Bultmann, the sacrificial
elements in Paul's theology were unpalatable remnants of the 'Old
Testament-Jewish tradition'. Léon-Dufour is still more squeamish
about the blood of Jesus. 'We must carefully refrain from regarding
this "blood" from the perspective of the bloody sacrifices in other
religions, or even within the framework of Jewish sacrifices', he
cautions.[49] 'To give expression to Christ's death there is no need now
to refer to the sacrifices of the Old Testament, except to note their
end, their disappearance ...'[50] Léon-Dufour is pained by a common
tendency among Christians, loosely based on a sacrificial reading of
Paul,[51] to speak 'of sin's "offence" against God and of God's
intention to punish and to chastise', on the one hand, and 'of
"reparation", of "satisfaction", and of "merit" by which the human
Jesus "satisfied" divine justice', on the other hand.[52] This leads to a
'distressing attribution' to God of 'inadmissible dispositions'.[53] Although Léon-Dufour does not say so explicitly, the dispositions in
question are those of a cruel despot who keeps his fearful subjects in
check through the threat of frightful physical punishment – the sort
of despot who features prominently in the early chapters of *Discipline and Punish*. Interestingly, the public executions by torture in
eighteenth-century France led to the precise phenomenon that Léon-
Dufour deplores, an attribution to the sovereign of 'inadmissible
dispositions'. Foucault writes: 'It was as if the punishment was
thought to equal, if not to exceed, in savagery the crime itself, to
accustom the spectators to a ferocity from which one wished to
divert them, ... to make the executioner resemble a criminal, judges

murderers....'[54] Léon-Dufour's God is not given to theatrical displays of power. A 'healthy understanding of Jesus' death' would emphasize instead its transformative potential, how it is 'active' in the believer through baptism and the eucharist 'so that it exercises its influence in ordinary life'.[55] Once again, as in the eighteenth-century rhetoric of judicial reform, the recommended shift of emphasis is from corporal punishment ('painful to a more or less horrible degree', as one contemporary glossed it)[56] to internal reform leading to a transformation of everyday behaviour.

'The key to a tradition often lies in what it excludes ...' What is it that the transformational interpretation of the crucifixion excludes? Is it the issue of power, an issue all too close to the surface in the punitive interpretation, the power of one person over the body of another, a power never more evident than in the relationship of the torturer to the victim – and never more disturbing, perhaps, than when the torturer is God and the victim his Son? But what if the transformation of the believer were merely a more *efficient* exercise of power, still exercised on the body but now reaching into the psyche as well to fashion acceptable thoughts and attitudes yielding acceptable behaviour, of power absolutized to a degree unimaginable even in a situation of extreme physical torture? This, above all, is the question that *Discipline and Punish* prompts us to ask.

Discipline and Discipleship

Are they ministers of Christ? ... I am a better one: with far greater labours, far more imprisonments, with countless floggings, and often near death. Five time I have received from the Jews the forty lashes minus one. Three time I was beaten with rods.

II Corinthians 11.23–25

Let us rephrase the question: What if the crucified Jesus, as interpreted by Paul, were actually God's own (pri)son? The prison would contain a courtyard, and the courtyard would be dominated by a scaffold. Needless to say, Paul's gospel of reform cannot simply be equated with the judicial reforms of the eighteenth century. For the latter, the punitive liturgy of public torture had to be consigned once and for all to history. But for Paul, discipline remains indissolubly bound up with atrocity. Each believer must be subjected to public execution by torture: 'Do you not know that all of us who have been

baptized into Christ Jesus were baptized into his death?' (Rom. 6.3).
Paul refuses to separate torture from reform (cf. I Cor. 1.18ff.; Gal.
2.19–21). Unless the believer is tortured to death in the (pri)son, he
or she cannot be rehabilitated: 'We know that our old self was
crucified with him so that the sinful body might be destroyed [*hina
katargēthē to sōma tēs hamartias*]' (Rom. 6.6; cf. Gal. 5.24).

Of course, Christian discipline is also bound up with power: 'the
kingdom of God does not consist in talk but in power [*en dunamei*]'
(I Cor. 4.20). How is this power exercised and who is entitled to
exercise it? Foucault's views on power may be pertinent here. 'In
thinking of the mechanisms of power,' he explains, 'I am thinking ...
of its capillary forms of existence, the point where power reaches
into the very grain of individuals, touches their bodies ...'[57] For
Foucault, 'nothing is more material, physical, corporal than the
exercise of power'[58] – and for Paul, too, seemingly. As Elizabeth A.
Castelli has remarked of I Corinthians, 'the human body provides a
central series of images and themes for this text ... Food practices
and sexuality occupy fully half of the letter's content ... It is also the
case that explicit language about authority and power is used most
frequently in the discussion of bodily practices ...'[59]

Discipline has only one purpose, according to Foucault: the
production of 'docile bodies'.[60] 'A body is docile that may be
subjected, used, transformed and improved', says Foucault.[61] 'I
punish my body and enslave [*doulagōgō*] it', says Paul (I Cor. 9.27).
Indeed, the docility engendered by discipline is precisely that of the
slave.[62] 'Whoever was free when called is a slave [*doulos*] of Christ',
says Paul (I Cor. 7.22), he himself being no exception (Rom. 1.1; cf.
Phil. 1.1). Of course, there are slaves and 'slaves' (cf. I Cor. 7.21–24;
Philemon 15–16), and Paul is in the parenthesized category. Even
among 'slaves', moreover, a strict hierarchy is observed; the man is
the 'head' [*kephalē*] of the woman, for example, even as Christ is the
'head' of the man (I Cor. 11.3; 14.34). Christ himself is also a
subject: 'When all things are subjected to him, then the Son himself
will also be subjected to the one who put all things in subjection
under him' (I Cor. 15.28; cf. 11.3). Even when Jesus' crucifixion is
interpreted as a means toward internalized discipline, then, rather
than as retributive punishment for sin (and Paul is not uncomfortable with the latter interpretation), absolute power continues to be
attributed to a monarchical God. The question that inevitably arises
is, Who stands to benefit from this attribution? To appeal to one's

own exemplary subjection to a conveniently absent authority in order to legitimate the subjection of others is a strategy as ancient as it is suspect. 'Be imitators [*mimētai*] of me, as I am of Christ', says Paul (I Cor. 11.1; cf. I Cor. 4.16; I Thess. 1.6). Above all, imitate my obedience by obeying me (cf. I Cor. 11.16; 14.37–38).[63]

'It has often been said that Christianity brought into being a code of ethics fundamentally different from that of the ancient world', writes Foucault, adding that what is less often noted is that Christianity 'spread new power relations throughout the ancient world'.[64] This new form of power Foucault terms *pastoral power*. It 'is not merely a form of power which commands; it must also be prepared to sacrifice itself for the life and salvation of the flock. Therefore, it is different from royal power, which demands a sacrifice from its subjects to save the throne.'[65] Ultimately, for Foucault, 'this form of power cannot be exercised without knowing the inside of people's minds, without exploring their souls, without making them reveal their innermost secrets. It implies a knowledge of the conscience and an ability to direct it.'[66] Foucault is thinking particularly of the sacrament of penance here,[67] which assumed the status of a Christian obligation only after the Fourth Lateran Council in 1215 CE, but which is deeply rooted in the ancient Jewish conception of an all-seeing God who 'searches' and 'tests' the human heart, exposing its innermost secrets (cf. I Sam. 16.7; I Kings 8.39; I Chron. 28.9; Pss. 17.3; 26.2; 44.21; 139.1–2, 23; Prov. 15.11; Jer. 11.20; 12.3; 17.10). Although this tradition does not achieve anything like its full flowering in Paul – that will have to await the institution of private confession – Paul does allude frequently to it (e.g., Rom. 2.16, 29; 8.27; I Cor. 4.5; 14.25). In time, Paul's ecclesiastical descendants will appropriate for themselves the divine privilege of laying bare the human soul. 'Since the Middle Ages at least, Western societies have established the confession as one of the main rituals we rely on for the production of truth …'[68] But this form of discipline too will be closely bound up with atrocity. 'One confesses – or is forced to confess. When it is not spontaneous or dictated by some internal imperative, the confession is wrung from a person by violence or threat; it is driven from its hiding place in the soul, or extracted from the body. Since the Middle Ages, torture has accompanied it like a shadow, and supported it when it could go no further: the dark twins.'[69]

Eventually, Foucault argues, this coercive obsession with the state

132

of the soul becomes the soul of the modern state. His hypothesis is that 'the modern Western state has integrated in a new political shape, an old power technique', namely, pastoral power, with its investment in the regulation of the individual's inner existence.[70] This power technique, 'which over centuries – for more than a millennium – had been linked to a defined religious institution, suddenly spread out into the whole social body; it found support in a multitude of institutions'.[71]

As it happens, these are the same institutions of surveillance and control that Foucault has repeatedly attacked in his writings. Of course, they are not necessarily the institutions that ordinarily leap to mind in this connection – the KGB, the CIA, etc. As we have seen, power is at its most insidious and efficient, for Foucault, precisely when its workings are effaced – when its brow is furrowed with humanitarian concern, when its voice is warm with Christian compassion, when its menace is masked even, or especially, from itself. The institutions that Foucault has taken aim at in his writings, therefore, are particularly those in which power wears a white coat and a professional smile. They include psychiatry, the secular sacrament of penance, and the target of his first major work, *Madness and Civilization*;[72] modern medicine, which exposes the innermost secrets of the human body to the scientific gaze, and the subject of his next book, *The Birth of the Clinic*;[73] the social sciences, which likewise turn the human subject into an object of scientific scrutiny, and the target of his third major work, *The Order of Things*;[74] modern methods of dealing with delinquency and criminality, the subject of *Discipline and Punish*; and the modern policing of sexual 'normality', the subject of the first volume of his *History of Sexuality*.

Foucault once confessed in an interview: 'A nightmare has pursued me since childhood: I have under my eyes a text that I can't read, or of which only a tiny part can be deciphered; I pretend to read it, but I know that I'm inventing ...'[75] Foucault tempts us to invent in our turn, to write preludes and sequels to his own surreal historical narrative, one in which the melancholy murmur of a mediaeval penitential liturgy is heard echoing through the contemporary halls of science, of medicine, and of justice – the public dismemberment of the body of the deviant having been displaced by strategies of social control that seem to grow ever lighter the deeper they extend into each of us.[76]

Epilogue

I recall that each ornate confessional in the Redemptorist church displayed, deep in its sombre interior, the effigy of a tortured man, and that the column of confessionals was itself flanked by the fourteen Stations of the Cross, each one ornate and imposing, the spectacle of atrocity being inseparable, as I now realize, from the spectacle of docility, 'the quiet game of the well behaved'.[77]

Notes

1. Page duBois, *Torture and Truth*, New York: Routledge 1991.
2. Martin Hengel, *Crucifixion in the Ancient World and the Folly of the Message of the Cross*, trans. John Bowden, London: SCM Press and Philadelphia: Fortress Press 1977. When I tracked down this book in the college library I was surprised to find that it was not shelved in the religion section, as I had expected, but in a corner of the history section devoted to torture. Hengel's monograph was flanked by illustrated treatises on mediaeval torture, on the one hand, and Amnesty International reports, on the other.
3. The German edition of the work bore the Latin title *Mors turpissima crucis*, 'the utterly vile death of the cross', a quotation from Origen (*Comm. Matt.* 27.22). Josephus similarly deemed crucifixion 'the most wretched of deaths' (*JW* 7.203), while Cicero called it 'that most cruel and disgusting penalty', and 'the ultimate punishment' (*Verr.* 2.5.165, 168).
4. Ibid., 87.
5. Ibid., 25.
6. Michel Foucault, *Discipline and Punish: The Birth of the Prison*, trans. Alan Sheridan, New York: Vintage Books 1977, 3.
7. Ibid.
8. Ibid., 73.
9. Ibid., 74.
10. Hayden White, 'Michel Foucault', in *Structuralism and Since: From Lévi-Strauss to Derrida*, ed. John Sturrock, Oxford: Oxford University Press, 1979, 106.
11. Michel Foucault, 'On Power', in *Politics, Philosophy, Culture: Interviews and Other Writings 1977–1984*, ed. Lawrence D. Kritzman, trans. Alan Sheridan et al., New York: Routledge 1988, 101.
12. DuBois, *Torture and Truth*, 153.
13. Foucault, *Discipline and Punish*, 307.

14. DuBois, *Torture and Truth*, 154.
15. Ibid. Foucault himself was not unaware of this: 'I could perfectly well call my subject [in *Discipline and Punish*] the history of penal policy in France – alone' ('Questions on Geography', in *Power/Knowledge: Selected Interviews and Other Writings 1972–1977*, ed. Colin Gordon, trans. Colin Gordon et al., New York: Pantheon Books 1980, 67).
16. Cf. DuBois, *Torture and Truth*, 154–57.
17. Hengel, *Crucifixion*, 88.
18. Ibid., 87.
19. Whether 'the rulers of this age' in I Cor. 2.8 are to be understood as human authorities, supernatural authorities (cf. Col. 2.15), or a combination of both does not substantially affect the issue.
20. See Frances M. Young, *The Use of Sacrificial Ideas in Greek Christian Writers from the New Testament to John Chrysostom*, Cambridge, MA: Philadelphia Patristic Foundation 1979.
21. It has been adopted by the Roman Catholic magisterium although 'not actually defined' (Karl Rahner and Herbert Vorgrimler, *Dictionary of Theology*, trans. Richard Strachan et al., 2nd ed.; New York: Crossroad 1981, 463).
22. Gustaf Aulén, *Christus Victor: An Historical Study of the Three Main Types of the Idea of the Atonement*, trans. A.G. Herbert, London: SPCK 1931; New York: Macmillan 1940, 18.
23. Ibid., 18–19. Salient statements of the Reformers on the atonement are reproduced in Pierre Grelot, *Péché originel et rédemption examinés à partir de l'Epître aux Romains. Essai Théologiques*, Paris: Declée 1973, 205ff.
24. From the Introduction to St Anselm, *Proslogium; Monologium; an Appendix in Behalf of the Fool by Gaunilon; and Cur Deus Homo*, trans. Sidney Norton Deane and James Gardiner Vose, La Salle, IL: Open Court 1951, viii.
25. Hubert L. Dreyfus and Paul Rabinow, *Michel Foucault: Beyond Structuralism and Hermeneutics*, 2nd ed.; Chicago: University of Chicago Press 1983, 145.
26. Madan Sarup, 'Foucault and the Social Sciences', in *An Introductory Guide to Post-Structuralism and Postmodernism*, Athens: University of Georgia Press 1989, 74. Writing of this period, Foucault himself uses language such as the following: 'torture forms part of a ritual. It is an element in the liturgy of punishment' (*Discipline and Punishment*, 34).
27. Douglas Moo, *Romans 1–8*, Wycliffe Exegetical Commentary; Chicago: Moody Press 1991, 94. He singles out C.H. Dodd (*The Epistle of Paul to the Romans*, Moffatt New Testament Commentary; Hodder & Stoughton 1932) as representative of this influential school of

thought. A more current example would be James D.G. Dunn, for whom Paul's conception of God's wrath is a highly nuanced affair, transcending the commonplace notions of 'divine indignation' and 'judicial anger against evil', not to mention divine vengeance (*Romans 1–8*, Word Biblical Commentary 38A; Dallas: Word Books 1988, 54–55, 70–71).

28. Anders Nygren, *Commentary on Romans*, Philadelphia: Fortress Press 1949, 98.

29. So too Xavier Léon-Dufour, whose *Life and Death in the New Testament* (trans. Terrence Prendergast; San Francisco: Harper & Row 1986) I shall briefly discuss below. This embarrassment is less pronounced in other New Testament studies that deal with the atonement, such as Vincent Taylor, *The Atonement in New Testament Teaching*, London: Epworth 1940; Martin Hengel, *The Atonement: The Origins of the Doctrine in the New Testament*, trans. John Bowden, London: SCM Press and Philadelphia: Fortress Press 1981; and Kenneth Grayston, *Dying, We Live: A New Enquiry into the Death of Christ in the New Testament*, London: Darton, Longman & Todd, 1990.

30. The following discussion is indebted to Robert H. Gundry's critique of Bultmann in his *Soma in Biblical Theology: With Emphasis on Pauline Anthropology*, New York: Cambridge University Press 1976; see esp. 206–9.

31. Rudolf Bultmann, *Theology of the New Testament*, trans. Kendrick Grobel, London: SCM Press and New York: Charles Scribner's Son 1951, vol. 1, 249.

32. Ibid., 249.

33. Ibid., 246.

34. Ibid., 246, his emphasis.

35. Ibid., 295. According to Bultmann, this view underlies the following passages: Rom. 3.25ff.; 5.9; I Cor. 11.24ff.; I Cor. 15.3; II Cor. 5.14; cf. Rom. 4.25; 5.6, 8; 8.32; 14.15; Gal. 1.4; 2.20; I Thess. 5.10.

36. Ibid., 296.

37. Ibid.

38. Ibid.

39. Rudolf Bultmann, 'New Testament and Mythology', in *Kerygma and Myth: A Theological Debate*, ed. Hans Werner Bartsch, trans. Reginald H. Fuller, London: SPCK 1957; New York: Harper & Row 1961, 7.

40. Bultmann, *Theology of the New Testament*, vol. 1, 296.

41. Ibid., 297–98, his emphasis.

42. Bultmann, 'New Testament and Mythology', 5.

43. Sarup, 'Foucault and the Social Sciences', 74.

44. This corresponds roughly to the 'subjective' doctrine of the atonement, commonly associated with Abelard, and distinguished from Anselm's

'objective' doctrine. The former term 'is used to describe a doctrine which explains the Atonement as consisting essentially in a change taking place in men rather than a changed attitude on the part of God' (Aulén, *Christus Victor*, 18). The subjective doctrine came into prominence during the Enlightenment (when, as we have seen, the practice of public execution by torture was also being questioned): 'A "more human" idea of the Atonement was propounded to replace the accepted "juridical" treatment ... The doctrine of retributive punishment was scouted, for punishment could only be ameliorative' (ibid., 150).

Interestingly, around the same time, an aspect of the traditional doctrine of hell, one defended by Augustine, Aquinas, and Peter of Lombardy among others, was gradually dropped. This was the idea 'that part of the happiness of the blessed consists in contemplating the torments of the damned [cf. Rev. 14.9–10; Luke 16: 23–26; Isa. 66.24]. This sight gives them joy because it is a manifestation of God's justice and hatred of sin ...' (D.P. Walker, *The Decline of Hell: Seventeenth-Century Discussions of Eternal Torment*, Chicago: University of Chicago Press 1964, 29).

45. Bultmann, 'New Testament and Mythology', 32, his emphasis. This sentiment is, of course, a commonplace of Pauline studies.
46. Howard Eilberg-Schwartz, *The Savage in Judaism: An Anthropology of Israelite Religion and Ancient Judaism*, Bloomington and Indianapolis: Indiana University Press 1990, 25.
47. Ibid., 31–86.
48. Ibid., 55.
49. Léon-Dufour, *Life and Death in the New Testament*, 189.
50. Ibid., 190.
51. A 'Paul' who is also the author of Hebrews.
52. Léon-Dufour, *Life and Death in the New Testament*, 192.
53. Ibid.
54. Foucault, *Discipline and Punish*, 9.
55. Léon-Dufour, *Life and Death in the New Testament*, 192. Compare Dunn on Rom. 6.4: 'We should note at once how quickly Paul jumps from a deep theological concept (union with Christ in his death) to talk of daily conduct. For Paul, evidently, *the character of daily conduct is actually determined by these deeper realities*, the hidden self-understandings and sources of strength which come to expression in day-to-day living. The proof of such deeper realities is not some profound mystical experience but the daily decisions of everyday relationships and responsibilities' (*Romans 1–8*, 330, his emphasis).
56. Quoted in Foucault, *Discipline and Punish*, 33.
57. Foucault, 'Prison Talk', in *Power/Knowledge*, 39.
58. Foucault, 'Body/Power', in *Power/Knowledge*, 57–58.

59. Elizabeth A. Castelli, 'Interpretations of Power in 1 Corinthians', *Semeia* 54 (1991): 209.

60. Cf. Foucault, *Discipline and Punish*, 135–69.

61. Ibid., 136.

62. Just as crucifixion in the Roman world was, above all, 'the slaves' punishment' (Cicero, *Verr.* 2.5.169). Through Jesus' crucifixion, the Christian slave is disciplined and kept in line.

63. Elizabeth Castelli builds a Foucaultian reading of Paul on this motif; see *Imitating Paul: A Discourse of Power*, Literary Currents in Biblical Interpretation; Louisville: Westminster/John Knox Press 1991.

64. Foucault, 'The Subject and Power', in Dreyfus and Rabinow, *Michel Foucault*, 214.

65. Ibid.

66. Ibid. Further on pastoral power, see Foucault, 'Politics and Reason', in *Politics, Philosophy, Culture*, 60ff.

67. This is clear from Foucault, 'Technologies of the Self', in *Technologies of the Self: A Seminar with Michel Foucault*, ed. Luther H. Martin, Huck Gutman, and Patrick H. Hutton, Amherst: University of Massachusetts Press 1988, 40–41.

68. Michel Foucault, *The History of Sexuality. Volume 1: An Introduction*, trans. Robert Hurley, New York: Vintage Books 1978, 58.

69. Ibid., 59.

70. Foucault, 'The Subject and Power', 213. The symbol of the modern state, for Foucault, or better, of the 'disciplinary society', is the *Panopticon*, Jeremy Bentham's utopian design for the perfect disciplinary institution. In the Panopticon, the inmates would be totally and permanently visible to supervisors who themselves would normally be invisible (*Discipline and Punish*, 195–228). On the connections between the Panopticon and the all-seeing God of Judaeo-Christianity, see Stephen D. Moore, *Mark and Luke in Poststructuralist Perspectives: Jesus Begins to Write*, New Haven: Yale University Press 1992, 129–44.

71. Foucault, 'The Subject and Power', 215.

72. Michel Foucault, *Madness and Civilization: A History of Insanity in the Age of Reason*, trans. Richard Howard, New York: Pantheon Books 1965.

73. Michel Foucault, *The Birth of the Clinic: An Archaeology of Medical Perception*, trans. Alan Sheridan, New York: Pantheon Books 1973.

74. Michel Foucault, *The Order of Things: An Archaeology of the Human Sciences*, trans. anon., New York: Pantheon Books 1970.

75. Michel Foucault, 'The Discourse of History', in *Foucault Live (Interviews, 1966–84)*, ed. Sylvere Lotringer, trans. John Johnson, New York: Semiotext(e) 1989, 25.

76. Its touch is lightest of all in the case of television, a 'disciplinary

God's Own (Pri)son

technology' that Foucault never examined. The obverse of Paul's pan-
optic God, television's single blind eye polices and controls, not by being
all-seeing, but by being seen by all.
77. Foucault, *Discipline and Punish*, 69.

7

Early Christianity and the Sociology of the Sect

Stephen C. Barton

Introduction

A collection of essays on 'New Directions for Biblical Studies' would be incomplete without some attempt to address and evaluate the wave of studies which, over the past two decades, have used models and methods from the social sciences to interpret the biblical literature.[1] This is a very large field already, so we need to narrow our focus. Even if we confine ourselves to the New Testament alone, the mass of secondary literature is very considerable, as several bibliographical essays show;[2] and there exist already a number of competent, book-length introductions to the field, such as those by Bruce Malina (1981), Derek Tidball (1983), Howard Clark Kee (1989), and most recently, Bengt Holmberg (1990).[3]

As a way through, therefore, I have chosen to focus on one particular issue in the social-scientific interpretation of the New Testament – namely, the appropriateness or otherwise of describing early Christianity as a 'sect'. Several factors explain – even if they do not justify – my choice. First, as will become clear, the application of the sociological model of the sect to various aspects of early Christianity is a commonplace now. Whether the text under examination is a gospel or an epistle or an apocalypse, its social setting invariably attracts the label, 'sectarian'. Perhaps this is an opportune time to test this remarkably widely-held consensus to see whether or not its foundations are secure.[4]

Second, the sect model has a distinguished pedigree, both in the social sciences and in the historiography of early Christianity. So this is no hermeneutical 'fly-by-night' to which we are giving our attention. On the contrary, the sociology of sects is a century old at least, and boasts names like Max Weber, Ernst Troeltsch, Georg Simmel, H. Richard Niebuhr, and more recently, Werner Stark and Bryan Wilson.[5] The discussion has a history, therefore; and it will be important to see whether or not an awareness of that history informs accounts given by New Testament scholars of early Christianity as sectarian.

Third, to label early Christianity as a sect is to employ a category which is not native to the first Christians themselves. A twentieth-century Western, social science category is being applied to a phenomenon of the first-century Mediterranean world. This is not objectionable in itself. On the contrary, we do this all the time as a way of making greater sense of the past or of cultures other than our own in terms which are intelligible to us. Nevertheless, it is important to recognize that such categories – etic (outsider) rather than emic (insider), to use the anthropological jargon – are likely to be distorting of what they describe, as well as illuminating, depending on where resides the final court of appeal.[6] In a nutshell, interpretations of early Christianity as a sect are likely to tell us as much about ourselves as interpreters as about the first Christians and their literary deposit. So the present paper is a case-study in interpretation which may be of interest not only to students of early Christianity and its social forms, but also to students of the art of interpretation itself. To put the matter pointedly: Do interpreters of early Christianity as a sect find what they are looking for already?

Early Christianity as a Sect?

Perhaps the best way to proceed is to look critically at specific accounts of early Christianity as sectarian. This will give some indication of how strong is the present consensus that the first Christians did constitute a sectarian movement. It will provide also a basis for judging some of the promise and pitfalls of this kind of sociological analysis.[7]

1. Robin Scroggs on the Jesus movement

A good place to begin is Robin Scroggs' wide-ranging essay of 1975, 'The Earliest Christian Communities as Sectarian Movement'.[8] Here

Scroggs claims that the sect model has never previously been applied in detail to the emergence of Christianity, and states his thesis thus:

> It is my conviction that the community called into existence by Jesus fulfills the essential characteristics of the religious sect, as defined by recent sociological analyses. Should this prove so, then the sect model provides us with a new perspective from which to view our material, one which will help gestalt the fragmentary data, and which will illumine the cares and concerns of the people who were attracted to Jesus and who formed the nucleus of the Christian communities. It will help us understand the quality of the experience in these communities.[9]

Scroggs then identifies seven characteristics of the sect as an ideal type before going on to show how the early Christian communities in fact exhibited these traits. The traits are that the sect (*a*) originates in protest against economic and societal repression, (*b*) rejects the values and ideology of the establishment, (*c*) adopts a counter-cultural, egalitarian ethos according to which status distinctions in 'the world' are left behind, (*d*) offers adherents love and acceptance not found outside, (*e*) exists as a voluntary association to which members belong by conviction and conversion rather than by birth, (*f*) demands total commitment maintained by group discipline, and (*g*) is often adventist or apocalyptic in its orientation on history.[10] Setting aside the Acts of the Apostles as 'late, tendentious, and offer[ing] few traditions that can be sociologically evaluated',[11] and disregarding Paul's letters as well, Scroggs focusses on the gospel traditions, and finds in them evidence of the seven characteristics of the sect he has just elaborated. Jesus was the leader of a protest movement of the predominantly socially and economically dispossessed; the movement he inaugurated rejected and was in turn rejected by society-at-large and by the official establishment; within the movement, communal life was organized on strongly egalitarian, anti-hierarchical lines, and members found love and mutual acceptance; membership was voluntary and totally demanding; and so on.[12] So Scroggs concludes:

> [T]he earliest church meets all the essential characteristics of the religious sect.... The use I have made of Synoptic pericopae in this paper illustrates how the gestalt changes the way the material is viewed. The church becomes from this perspective not a theo-

logical seminary but a group of people who have experienced the hurt of the world and the healing of communal acceptance. The perspective ... helps us to see that the church in its own way dealt with the problems individuals faced in repressive social circumstances.[13]

What are we to make of this early stab at a sociological analysis of early Christianity in terms of the sect model? Its strength lies in its bold attempt to wrest the New Testament documents from what Scroggs sees as the narrow concerns of dogmatic theology or the romanticizing tendencies of Christian piety, and to show that these documents bear testimony to the often harrowing real-life situations of communities of believers trying to protest against or come to terms with the harsh political, economic and religious realities of life in the world of their time. Interpreting the early church in sectarian terms allows us to recapture the innovative, counter-cultural, protest dimension at the very core of the Christian heritage: and this may function as a corrective or rebuke to conservative religious establishments today. Says Scroggs: 'Traditional Christianity, full of support for law and order ... has lost all feeling for the sectarian protest of the earliest church. From the standpoint of sectarian reality, however, the death of Jesus offers a powerful symbolism for the outcast and alienated ...'[14]

But there are weaknesses to this kind of approach as well. Above all, it is quite clear from the article that Scroggs' sociological analysis is wedded to his own theological and ideological agenda. There is no sense in which Scroggs hides his light under a bushel on this score. In the second sentence of his essay, for example, he refers to 'the poison of over-theologizing which has been characteristic of so much New Testament scholarship during the neo-orthodox era'.[15] It is by no means coincidental that he finds the sect model so apposite for interpreting early Christianity, for his own ecclesiology is one of the church as a protest movement from below standing over against the conservative values of the establishment. Is it the case, then, that Scroggs has chosen a model to produce a result which he has arrived at already on other grounds? Do we not have here a classic example of the problem of the hermeneutical circle, and, if we are predisposed not to accept Scroggs' own theological and ecclesiological presuppositions, shall we not want to say that the hermeneutical circle is a vicious one? Will not those who suspect that sociological analysis generally is little more than an ideological tool of the political Left or Right have their suspicions confirmed? What claims to be explanatory turns out in practice to be a not-so-subtle ideological rhetoric.

Even if we accept that the sect model may throw new light on Christian origins, there are other weaknesses in Scroggs' analysis. Briefly, they are as follows. First, there is the problem of gross oversimplification. On the one hand, the idea of the sect itself is described in a very general and monolithic way, so that it is hardly surprising that the early church can be described as sectarian, especially when one begins to suspect that the characteristics of the ideal type have been taken from early Christianity in the first place! On the other hand, early Christianity is described also in a general and monolithic way as a peasant protest movement reacting against oppression and marginalization from an equally undifferentiated body called 'the establishment'. There is little sense in what Scroggs says of either the diversity of identity in early Christianity, or of the diversity – often of a quite sectarian kind, perhaps – within Judaism. So, as a tool of analysis, the sect model as used by Scroggs, seems to be a very blunt one indeed.

Second, if the sect as an ideal type is used to 'help gestalt the fragmentary data',[16] it functions also to block other data out. So general are the characteristics of the sect, so loaded are they with evaluative terms – like 'protest', 'counter-culture', 'egalitarian', 'love and acceptance', 'voluntary' and 'commitment' – that a powerful rhetoric may blind us to other data and other possibilities of interpretation. So, for example, Scroggs can do little with evidence that the socio-economic status and socio-ecological location of the early Christians was variable,[17] since his model assumes agrarian impoverishment and protest from below. His omission of the evidence of Acts is significant in this regard. Likewise, evidence that the early Christians shared the values, practices and prejudices of the society-at-large passes unmentioned. The admonition in Matt. 17.24–27 to continue to pay the temple tax does not sit easily with the anti-establishment sect model. Nor, in the same gospel, does the role diversity and status differentiation implied in what is said about Peter (cf. Matt. 16.17–19) or in what is said about the 'prophet' and 'scribe' (cf. Matt. 10.41; 13.52) fit well with the idea of the sect as egalitarian.

Third, early Christian beliefs and doctrines assume an epi-

144

phenomenal status in Scroggs' analysis. What 'really' matters are social and economic relations and the formation of communities of protest. In short, in reacting against what he sees as a kind of theological reductionism, Scroggs leaves little place for an early Christian theological consciousness at all. No one is likely to dispute Scroggs' claim that the early church was not a theological seminary, but it is highly questionable to imply that matters of doctrine, scriptural interpretation, spiritual discernment and (what we would call) ethics were not a constant focus of attention. Well before Scroggs' article, at least one ancient historian saw fit to write a major essay depicting the early Christians as a 'scholastic community'.[18] It is arguable that the designation 'scholastic community' does more justice to certain aspects, at least, of the evidence about early Christianity than does the designation 'sect'.

2. Wayne Meeks on the Fourth Gospel

We turn, next, from social scientific criticism of the Synoptic traditions to work done on the Fourth Gospel. Roughly contemporary with Robin Scroggs' work is an important and influential essay by Wayne Meeks, entitled, 'The Man from Heaven in Johannine Sectarianism', published in 1972.[19] Here Meeks argues that a major clue to the distinctiveness of this gospel – and of its discourses in particular – lies, not so much in *religionsgeschichtlich* factors to do with John's indebtedness or otherwise to gnosticism or heterodox Judaism, but in sociological factors to do with the kind of community to which the gospel is addressed. The distinctiveness of the discourses is to be sought, not so much in the history of ideas, as in the social function of the gospel's persistently riddling, repetitive, opaque, symbolic and mythological language. To outsiders – even sympathetic ones like Nicodemus – what Jesus says is a cause of misunderstanding and offence: to insiders it is divine revelation. Just as the Jesus of John is a stranger to the world and even to his own people, so too is the Johannine community. Meeks sums up his thesis thus:

> *The book functions for its readers in precisely the same way that the epiphany of its hero functions within its narratives and dialogues....* In telling the story of the Son of Man who came

down from heaven and then re-ascended after choosing a few of his own out of the world, the book defines and vindicates the existence of the community that evidently sees itself as unique, alien from its world, under attack, misunderstood, but living in unity with Christ and through him with God. It could hardly be regarded as a missionary tract, for we may imagine that only a very rare outsider would get past the barrier of its closed metaphorical system. It is a book for insiders.[20]

Meeks is not alone in his view that the Fourth Gospel betrays a sectarian, in-group consciousness. Amongst others who take this view we may cite J. Louis Martyn, Raymond Brown, Fernando Segovia and, most recently, David Rensberger.[21] D. Moody Smith reflects a widely held consensus when he says: 'it can probably be agreed that on any reading of the Gospel and Epistles there appears a sectarian consciousness, a sense of exclusiveness, a sharp delineation of the community from the world ... Comparisons with community consciousness in Qumran, which is likewise related to a fundamental dualism, are entirely apposite and to the point.'[22]

Interpreting the Johannine literature in sectarian terms has much to commend it. It helps to explain the vilification of 'the Jews' and the strong sense of mutual hostility between them and believers in Jesus. The hostility is so sharp and the possibility of accommodation so meagre because, like an argument in the family, each side knows the other only too well and the psycho-social stakes are too high. It helps also to make sense of the uncompromising exclusiveness of Johannine christology and soteriology. Now, Jesus exclusively is the way to the Father, not Torah. Now, true worship takes place neither on Mount Gerizim nor on Mount Zion, but 'in spirit and in truth' (John 4.19ff.). Now, the only temple where God is to be encountered is the temple of Jesus' own body. In fact, almost every major symbol of belonging as a Jew to the people of God – temple, Torah, festival calendar, sabbath observance, the land, the scriptures and the patriarchs – is displaced in a quite counter-cultural way by the Jesus of John. At the same time, the sect model makes intelligible the hints we are given of the ethos of the Johannine community, in spite of the absence of any explicit ecclesiology. I have in mind, for example, the strongly centripetal character of the love commandment; the emphasis on humility and equality in inter-personal relations dramatized in the episode of the footwashing (John 13.1–20); the predominant orientation of the Johannine symbols on nurture, sustenance, abiding and unity; the charismatic emphasis on the availability of the Spirit-Paraclete to the members of the group; and the overwhelmingly pessimistic outlook on relations with 'the world' and its institutional manifestations, whether Jewish or Roman.

What distinguishes Meeks' use of social science categories from that of Scroggs? Primarily the fact that, in Meeks' hands the social science tools are used in a much more refined way, such that explanation of the data is not confused with political and religious advocacy. Instead of imposing a rather undifferentiated sect model on a similarly undifferentiated range of gospel textual data, Meeks begins with a widely-recognized literary and hermeneutical puzzle in Johannine studies (i.e., how to explain the 'special patterns of language' of the Johannine Christ, including the motif of the ascending and descending redeemer), demonstrates the inadequacy of previous, *religionsgeschichtlich* attempts to solve the puzzle, and then draws in perspectives from the structuralist anthropology of Edmund Leach in order to suggest that a solution to the puzzle can be found if the model of interpretation shifts from the theological and historical to the sociological, to how mythological language functions in the communities who use it. Meeks says: 'It is only, therefore, by paying attention to the underlying structure of the components in a system of myths that an interpreter can "hear" what the myths are "saying" or, to put it another way, can discover the function which the myths have within the group in which they are at home. It is astonishing that attempts to solve the Johannine puzzle have almost totally ignored the question of what *social* function the myth may have had.'[23] So Meeks uses a very specific social scientific tool of analysis to help resolve a very specific problem of interpretation. And he chooses a tool of analysis which has, arguably, a natural congruence or compatibility with the literary puzzle he is working to solve. Unlike Scroggs, he resists the temptation to claim too much for his model or to try to do too much with it. The sociological dimension helpfully supplements the theological and historical dimensions without being in such danger of reducing them to the epiphenomenal.[24]

Nevertheless, having seen how strong is the sect model in relation to John, how suggestive it is for the attempt of the historical and sociological imagination to relate Johannine christology to Johannine community, it is important also to highlight some of the weaknesses, problems or unanswered questions. There is, for example, the persistent problem, not at all unique to the interpretation of John, of drawing sociological inferences from a very small literary deposit, even if we include the Johannine epistles as well. Meeks' claim, extended to an extreme degree by Raymond Brown in *The Community of the Beloved Disciple*, that the story of the Johannine Jesus is, in effect, a cypher for the history and sociology of the Johannine community is creative and imaginative, certainly. But it must be questioned whether or not interpreting the gospel narrative as a kind of allegory of the Johannine community runs too great a risk of finding what is not there or what, by the nature of the evidence, cannot be found.

Certainly, the evidence is ambiguous, and that alone should give us reason for caution. Meeks makes a lot, for example, of the sectarian, 'us-versus-them', consciousness which can be read off the encounter between Jesus and Nicodemus, in John 3.[25] But it may be questioned whether Nicodemus is cast in the outsider role which Meeks attributes to him; whether also he plays the role of an uncomprehending fool – any more, say, than a Samaritan woman or a Thomas or a Peter; and whether what is being conveyed in the dialogue is only that Jesus is incomprehensible, as Meeks claims. A more sympathetic reading is certainly possible, and if it is, then a crack begins to appear in Meeks' sectarian edifice. Notably, Raymond Brown, who is at most points sympathetic to Meeks' approach, says of Nicodemus that '[his] role is not to illustrate or personify the attitudes of a contemporary group in the Johannine experience, but to show how some who were attracted to Jesus did not immediately understand him.'[26]

Doubt may also be cast on Meeks' claim that the Fourth Gospel shows all the signs of being a 'book for insiders', since 'only a very rare outsider would get past the barrier of its closed metaphorical system.'[27] This strikes me as a *tour de force*. On this view, it is a wonder that anyone made it into the Johannine community at all! Are metaphors like *logos*, light, bread, living water, good shepherd, true vine, Son of God, and so on – each of them with deep roots in the biblical and Jewish traditions and not without a certain currency in the wider Hellenistic milieu, either – as opaque as Meeks makes them out to be? If they are not, and if we recall in addition the strong, universalizing missionary thrust of John, then a further crack appears in Meeks' sociological interpretation.

An important caution is constituted also by Martin Hengel's recent book, *The Johannine Question*.[28] Whereas Meeks insists in his essay that 'the Johannine literature is the product not of a lone genius but of a community or group of communities that evidently persisted with some consistent identity over a considerable span of time',[29] Hengel argues that a single theological genius does indeed lie behind the Johannine corpus and that claims that the Fourth Gospel is somehow a community product are spurious. Hengel does not deny that the gospel and epistles took shape in a communal context. For Hengel, however, this context is best understood as a school of disciples over which John the elder presided for many years. It is not some anonymous sectarian consciousness that explains the distinctiveness of the Johannine material, therefore, but the creative theological activity of John. Says Hengel:

> Here, then, was a towering creative teacher who ventured with reference to the activity of the Spirit Paraclete to paint a quite different picture of the activity and proclamation of Jesus from that which we can see in the Synoptic tradition, and who introduced the post-Easter pre-existence and exaltation christology quite massively into his description of the Galilean master. We must assume that such a 'theologian', who was the opposite of a mere tradent did not fix the dialectical positions that he expressed at one stage once and for all as inviolable principles. In a specific situation of crisis he ventured to take up new focal points and even in some circumstances to correct himself – dialectically ... That such a teacher possessing the highest authority and with rich experience going back over two generations could react sharply and clearly to a controversy with a group of pupils who were adapting themselves to 'the spirit of the time' is not surprising. In his view these former pupils of his (and their seducers coming from outside) threatened the existence of his school and all the Christian communities in Asia.[30]

Significantly, Hengel makes no mention of Meeks' prior essay; and, as with our evaluation of Robin Scroggs' position, we are left wondering whether an alternative social model, more firmly grounded historically – that of the school – is not more convincing than that of the religious sect. Be that as it may, Hengel's study is a powerful reminder that Meeks' basically functionalist sociological interpretation shows a tendency towards determinism in its account of the relation between text and community and that it may be in danger of leaving insufficient room for the role of the creative individual, the evangelist himself.[31]

Interestingly, C.K. Barrett, in the second edition of his massive commentary on John (published in 1978), does not refer to Meeks' essay either (even though he does make wide use of Meeks' 1967 monograph, *The Prophet-King*). I do not know why this is so. Perhaps it has something to do with a reticence in British biblical scholarship – at least in the 1970s – to consider seriously the possibilities for interpretation opened up by the social sciences. Perhaps it is explained by the likelihood that Barrett holds to a different view of the purpose of John, where the emphasis lies not on the influence of sociological factors so much as on the primacy of theological considerations, especially the evangelist's concern to present a universalizing articulation of the Christian message. As Barrett says in a recent article on 'St John: Social Historian': 'Undoubtedly it is true that we must look to John for theology rather than sociology' – even though he immediately qualifies this by adding, 'But this is not quite all. Few works of theology are generated within an exclusively theological environment, and the great works of theology have owed a good deal to their social environment.'[32] That Barrett's position seems to be shifting is reflected in his essay of 1989 for the Eduard Lohse *Festschrift*, where he argues that we are likely to misunderstand the nature of Christian community (both then and now) unless we take seriously the fact that in its origins it had characteristics both of the school and of the conventicle or sect.[33] But this is still a long way – and with good reason, perhaps? – from a systematic attempt to interpret the Johannine corpus in terms of the sociology of sectarianism. Barrett appears to share with Hengel an overriding commitment to historical-contextual and traditio-historical method in a form which is exclusive of sociological analysis, even though, confusingly, both writers are prepared at times to use sociological terminology.[34]

A quite different kind of problem, not just with Meeks' interpretation but with sociological and social science interpretations generally, is whether or not interpreting John in the light of the sociology of the sect is a *distraction* in the reading of the text. This can be put in a number of ways. But in general terms, the point is that whether or not a method or model of interpretation is valid depends upon who is doing the reading and for what purpose.

Thus, from the viewpoint of certain forms of literary criticism, meaning lies within the narrative world of the text and is generated by the interaction of the reader and the autonomous text.[35] It is what happens on *this* side of the text which is important, not the pre-history of the text or claims about communities or whatever lying *behind* the text, claims which in any case have no way of being substantiated. On this view, Meeks' attempt to establish a correlation between distinctive and disturbing features of the gospel and a distinctive, sectarian community lying behind the gospel are futile and ill-conceived. Rather, the meaning of the text is literary and aesthetic. It does not depend on referentiality outside the text. The *aporiae* of the text are not an invitation to hypothesize about the social function of the language: they are a provocation to the imagination and aesthetic sensibilities of the reader.

Another way this objection can be put comes from the perspective of canonical criticism. According to this approach, what is of central validity for interpretation is the meaning of John's gospel as part of the canon of scripture and as the fourth of the four gospels. Here, what is important is to hear the written words in the way in which they have been heard traditionally in the life and worship of the church – as scripture and as gospel, the Word of God. Historical-exegetical methodology may contribute to the reader's appreciation of what the text meant to its original readers and listeners, and sociological analysis may help to explain the social and communal dialectic of which the text is somehow a product, but valid interpretation in terms of canonical criticism will accord these approaches subordinate status only and will acknowledge only an indirect relationship between canonical interpretation and historical or sociological interpretations. For what is important above all is hearing the text itself as scripture, addressed to every successive generation. Thus, Brevard Childs, in discussing John 9, a text which J. L. Martyn had made the centre of his very valuable attempt to reconstruct the history of the Johannine community 'behind' the text, says:

There is a wide consensus that Martyn has greatly illuminated the text by seeing it in relation to the expulsion from the synagogue ... Yet the crucial hermeneutical issue remains whether Martyn has correctly assessed the canonical function of this material within the final shape of the text ... I would argue that to take the canonical shape of the Gospel seriously is to recognize that the text's authoritative, kerygmatic witness is not identical with its historical development, but must be discerned from the literary form of the text itself.[36]

Now, it is unfair of course to judge Meeks' work and the work of others in the same line according to the criteria of models of interpretation which they do not employ. However, the more modest point is worth making: that what you see depends upon where you stand. As we have seen, from at least one literary critical point of view, the social function of a text in its original historical context is not relevant to the art of interpretation. And from the point of view of canonical criticism, the claim that the gospel of John betrays a sectarian consciousness is a distraction.

3. *Philip Esler on Luke-Acts*

Up until recently, Luke-Acts has been read either as a source for reconstructing the history of the early church or as a theological narrative designed to convey the evangelist's response to the doctrinal and existential dilemmas of his readers in the last decades of the first century. Attempts to give a sociological interpretation of Luke's two volumes have been almost entirely lacking. Philip Esler's book, *Community and Gospel in Luke-Acts: The Social and Political Motivations of Lucan Theology*, published in 1987,[37] is an important attempt to fill this gap, and heavy use is made of the sociology of sectarianism.

In company with redaction critics, Esler does not see Luke as a disinterested recorder of the story of Jesus and the early church. Nor, however, is Luke to be seen as some kind of armchair theologian 'who ponders over purely religious questions before issuing forth from his scriptorium to enlighten his fellow-Christians as to the correct attitude which they and their community should adopt to their social and political environment.'[38] Rather, as the book's subtitle suggests, Luke's is applied theology from the start, motivated by strong social and political interests, and written for a specific historical community whose needs are as much material as spiritual.

Using a method he calls 'socio-redaction criticism', Esler argues that Luke-Acts is best interpreted as written to provide legitimation for a Christian community whose relations with both the synagogue community and the wider Gentile society are fraught with the inevitable tensions and pressures arising from the Christian group's sectarian status.[39] Luke's theological narrative is given a strongly functionalist orientation: it legitimates and justifies the beliefs and practices of his group over against those of alternative social worlds which have been left behind at conversion. To quote Esler:

> One obvious way to provide the necessary reassurance, to legitimate the sectarian status of his *ekklesia*, was for Luke to write a history of the beginnings of Christianity which pinned the blame for the subsequent split firmly on the Jews, especially their leaders, and which explained and justified early developments, such as Jewish-Gentile table-fellowship, which were still of significance to his Christian contemporaries. From this viewpoint, history is important for Luke not, as Conzelmann suggests, as a replacement for the imminent expectation of the early church, but as a way of accounting for the present situation of his community. In other words, the key to Lucan historiography is not eschatology but etiology.[40]

The picture of Luke's community which emerges is a fascinating one. Contrary to the widely-held view that Luke's audience is Gentile, Esler argues that many in Luke's group are converts from Judaism or Gentile God-fearers. The reason for Luke's interest in table fellowship is to legitimate Jew-Gentile commensality in his community and to maintain Jew-Gentile cohesion in the face of strong opposition from synagogue Jews and Jewish Christians who see the practice as a threat to the identity of the Jewish *ethnos*. An essential *'sectarian strategy'* adopted by Luke is to defend the practice by appealing to, and re-writing, history. The great apostles, Peter and James, together with the Jerusalem church, are portrayed now by Luke as giving their backing to Jew-Gentile table fellowship.

A similar interpretation is placed upon other major themes of Luke-Acts – the status of the Jewish law, the place of the temple, attitudes to poverty and wealth, and attitudes to Roman authority. In each case, Esler argues that Luke's writing betrays strong political and social concerns which reflect both the socially and religiously mixed character of his community and its vulnerability as a sect to pressures from outside, above all from Judaism. In the chapter entitled, 'The Poor and the Rich', for instance, Esler argues that Luke developed a specific theology of poverty in order to address the problems of social stratification and economic disparity which threatened the fellowship; and Esler is sharp in his criticism of 'spiritualizing' and 'individualizing' interpretations. He says: 'That the Lucan Gospel imposes on the rich an indispensable requirement, quite at odds with the social values of their own society, to provide the destitute with food and other necessities of life in this world sounds the death-knell over all such interpretations of his theology as, affected by middle-class bias, present salvation as a reality reserved for the individual in the after-life.'[41]

Esler certainly gives the lie to Scroggs' curious claim, noted earlier, that Luke's writings, especially the Acts, offer few traditions that can be sociologically evaluated. The sect typology of Bryan Wilson and the model of sect development opened up by H. Richard Niebuhr are used to powerful explanatory effect in Esler's study to bring to our attention plausible social and political interests which lie behind and shape Luke-Acts.

However, once again, several critical questions need to be asked. First, there is the fundamental question of the purpose of Luke-Acts. Esler's interpretative method appears analogous to a 'hermeneutics of suspicion' approach to the text. Luke-Acts is not really an account of the past in order that his benefactor, Theophilus, may know the truth, as the author claims (cf. Luke 1.1–4). Rather, it is a coded address to a sectarian community, providing legitimation and justification for its alternative identity and lifestyle over against its parent body in Judaism. History is not history, but propaganda. Theology is not theology, but the ideology of an oppressed group. This may be putting the point too sharply. But the issue is an important one. It is the question of whether a social science model intended for purposes of sociological explanation is being used illegitimately to describe things from the native's point of view. Luke thought he was doing one thing: but in fact he was doing another.

Second, there is the related question, raised earlier, of the legitimacy of interpreting the text as a mirror of the (in this case) Lucan community. This question has been asked explicitly by another Lucan scholar who has worked also on a theme of interest to Esler – namely, the subject of the poor and the rich.[42] In his essay, 'On Finding the Lukan Community: A Cautious Cautionary Tale', published in 1979,[43] Luke Johnson makes a number of useful observations. First, not even in the interpretation of Paul's letters, occasional as they are and written to specific communities about identifiable problems, has there been unqualified success in drawing inferences from the letters about the social situation of the addressees. The Letter to the Romans is a particular case in point. Johnson puts it this way:

> The study of Paul's letters reminds us that even in documents of a genuinely occasional nature, not every element in the document is determined by the place, the people, or the occasion. Some things are there because of the demands of genre, the impetus of tradition, the logic of argumentation, the inertia of scriptural citations, and the idiosyncratic perceptions of the author. Responsible exegesis takes these factors into account *before* using passages as a mirror to community problems.[44]

Turning from Paul to mirror readings of the gospels, Johnson questions the common assumption that the pastoral and theological concerns of an evangelist are determined by a situation of crisis among his readers: 'Reading everything in the Gospel narratives as immediately addressed to a contemporary crisis reduces them to the level of cryptograms, and the evangelists to the level of tractarians.'[45] In regard to Luke-Acts in particular, he argues that the difficulties of mirror-reading are even more acute: the author's identity is unknown; the addressee is an individual not a church; due weight has to be given to the influence of the tradition and to Luke's professed intention to write an historical account; due weight has to be given also to differences between Luke's two volumes, differences which must complicate attempts to 'read off' the community from the text; and there is clear evidence of literary artifice in Luke's writing. Above all – and Johnson has applied this principle in his own study of the motif of possessions – it is the literary function of a theme or motif in the text which has to be taken most seriously: 'Given a fairly intricate and intelligible literary structure which, taken as a whole, conveys a coherent message, our *first* assumption with regard to individual parts within that structure should not be that they point to a specific community problem, but that they are in service to the larger literary goal of the author.'[46]

One or two final observations are worth making before we leave this particular case-study. Although Esler's work is much more sophisticated than the essay of Scroggs, it may not avoid completely some of the same pitfalls. Is the sect-church typology so wedded to the problems of modernity that it lacks a necessary affinity with the subject-matter to which it is being applied? It may be significant that the very recent collection of thirteen American essays on *The Social World of Luke-Acts: Models for Interpretation* makes no use at all of the sect model, preferring instead models primarily from the discipline of social anthropology.[47] Does the sect-church typology contain an implicit anti-Judaism, by casting Judaism as the monolithic, static, unreformed 'church' from which the Christian 'reform movement' separated and became a sect? Does it help the explanatory task to categorize the putative Lucan community as, not a thaumaturgic sect (although Luke-Acts arguably contains a stronger thaumaturgic interest than any other New Testament text), nor a revolutionary sect (although an imminent-end eschatology is not suppressed completely in Luke-Acts), but a conversionist sect where personal repentance and acceptance of the gospel accompanied (mostly) by baptism is at the heart of things? Do not such types -- general and approximate as they are – generate as many difficulties as they solve? And does their application to Luke-Acts not obscure the fact that the Greek word closest to what we mean by sect – namely, *hairesis* – is the word that Luke apparently chooses *not* to apply to Christianity, although well aware of its currency?[48] For Luke, the word *hodos* ('way') more aptly captures the identity and self-understanding of the new movement,[49] and *ekklesia* is the word he uses both for the local Christian community (e.g. Acts 5.11; 8.1, 3) and for all the local groups treated as a single whole (e.g. Acts 9.31; 20.28). Of course, it is inappropriate to accuse Esler of using categories for explanation which are not native and which a native would not recognize. The trouble with the category 'sect', however, is that, because of its roots in the Christian tradition, it hovers uneasily between being a native (emic) category, on the one hand, and a scientific (etic) category, on the other, so that it is difficult to be sure that it is being used in the value-neutral, scientific way claimed.

Conclusion

I have attempted in the foregoing case-studies, to give a critical assessment of three major essays which use the sociology of sects and sectarianism as a heuristic device for explaining the social dynamics of earliest Christianity. Other examples could have been chosen if for no other reason than to demonstrate how strong is the current consensus that the sect model throws important light on Christian origins.

On Matthew, there is J. Andrew Overman's recent book, *Matthew's Gospel and Formative Judaism*, which argues that this gospel represents the uncompromising response of a minority messianic sect to the growing dominance of what he calls 'formative Judaism' in the post-70 period, and that the whole period in Judaism between 165 BCE and 100 CE can be characterized as sectarian and factional.[50] On Mark, there is Howard Kee's monograph, *Community of the New Age*, which argues that Mark's audience is a missionary sect whose world-view is indebted to Jewish apocalyptic, and whose voluntaristic, inclusive and charismatic ethos is markedly at odds with dominant social mores.[51] On Paul, the work of Wayne Meeks is to the fore again, first in a stimulating essay on 'Group Boudaries in Pauline Christianity',[52] and most substantially in his book, *The First Urban Christians*[53] – although it is noteworthy that both works eschew systematic application of any one social science model out of preference for a more eclectic, pragmatic approach.[54] Much more systematic in applying the sect model to Paul is Francis Watson's *Paul, Judaism and the Gentiles: A Sociological Approach*, published in 1986.[55] Taking the application of the sect model further, from the Pauline into the post-Pauline literature and setting, is Margaret MacDonald's, *The Pauline Churches*.[56] This study uses the sociology of the sect to analyse and explain the churches' attitude to the world, and, like Esler on the Lucan community, sees the churches of Paul as a conversionist sect. According to MacDonald, the Pastoral Epistles represent the development, along Troeltschean sect-church lines, of a church-type community. Finally, but by no means exhaustively, there is J.H. Elliott's study of I Peter, which has been influential in sociological interpretations of the New Testament, not least in the works of Esler and MacDonald.[57] In *A Home for the Homeless*, Elliott argues that the addressees of I Peter are marginalized, 'resident aliens' (*paroikoi*) of Asia Minor whose conversion has increased the antagonism of the native residents towards them. They constitute, therefore, a conversionist sect in tension with the society-at-large. The strategy of the letter is to confirm the believers in their social and religious separation from outsiders and to emphasize their incorporation into an alternative family, the *oikos tou theou* ('household of God': cf. I Peter 2.5; 4.17).[58]

The overwhelming benefit of these studies is that they draw explicit attention to the kinds of social dynamics, factors and forces likely to have been influential in shaping the identity, self-understanding, thought-forms and behaviour of the earliest Christians. The sect model helps to explain why the New Testament texts show such persistent interest in defining and maintaining group boundaries, why priority is given to mission and conversion, why opponents are vilified, why ties of natural kinship are deprecated in favour of ties of spiritual kinship,[59] why exclusive claims are made for Jesus as 'messiah' and 'lord', why persecution and ostracism are the Christian believer's common experience, why an inner reform movement of Judaism very soon took on a separate identity, and so on.

However, while the consensus may be impressive, there are also grounds for caution. I mention two, by way of reiteration and conclusion. First, if it is possible to conclude that early Christianity of just about every hue was sectarian – Matthean as well as Marcan and Lucan, Johannine as well as Pauline and Petrine – we are forced to conclude that the category 'sect' has only relatively weak explanatory power.[60] Even with the kinds of refinements of the typology introduced by Bryan Wilson, it does not make possible the discrimination between the Christian groups – or within them – which is necessary to do justice to the evidence. Nor, it should be added, does it do justice to the wide variety of splinter groups and movements in first-century Judaism, let alone 'the complexities of religious life in the larger Roman Empire'.[61]

Second, the sect-church typology is prone to being made captive to ideological interests of one kind or another. This is due in part to the binary structure of the typology, which makes possible an implicit or explicit opposition between a kind of group or society which is viewed positively and another which is viewed negatively. An anti-establishment, left-wing ideology is likely to use 'sect' as a term of approbation. On the other hand, an establishment ideology is likely to use the term as a way of both identifying and marginalizing the enemy. In between, others may claim that they are using 'sect' in an objective, value-neutral way. But such interpreters, in all likelihood, are supporters of a clearly identifiable liberal ideological agenda and are the heirs of Enlightenment rationality. If there is any truth in the point I am making here, then the limitations, as well as the strengths, of the sect model are even more manifest. To put it another way, use of this model confronts us more clearly than is usually the case with the inevitably political nature of the act of interpretation.[62]

Notes

1. I am grateful to Joel B. Green of New College, Berkeley, for his helpful comments on this paper; and to Leslie Houlden and Francis Watson for the invitation to write and present it.
2. E.g. D.J. Harrington, 'Second Testament Exegesis and the Social Sciences: A Bibliography', *Biblical Theology Bulletin*, 18 (1988), 77–85; G. Theissen, Auswahlbibliographie zur Sozialgeschichte des Urchristentums', in his *Studien zur Soziologie des Urchristentums*, Tübingen: J.B. Mohr 1989, 331–370; and S.C. Barton, 'The Communal Dimension of Earliest Christianity: A Critical Survey of the Field', *Journal of Theological Studies*, 43 (1992), 399–427.
3. See B.J. Malina, *The New Testament World: Insights from Cultural Anthropology*, Atlanta: John Knox and London: SCM Press 1981; D. Tidball, *An Introduction to the Sociology of the New Testament*, Exeter: Paternoster Press 1983; H.C. Kee, *Knowing the Truth: A Sociological Approach to New Testament Interpretation*, Minneapolis: Fortress Press 1989; and B. Holmberg, *Sociology and the New Testament: An Appraisal*, Minneapolis: Fortress Press 1990.
4. See, most recently, the helpful essay by L. Michael White, 'Shifting Sectarian Boundaries in Early Christianity', *Bulletin of the John Rylands Library*, 70 (1988), 7–24.
5. For a useful survey of the sociological debate, see M. Hill, *A Sociology of Religion*, London: Heinemann 1973, 47–70. On the work of Wilson in particular, see D.E. Miller, 'Sectarianism and Secularization: The Work of Bryan Wilson', *Religious Studies Review*, 5/3 (1979), 161–174.
6. This point is made well in Mark Brett's recent book, *Biblical Criticism in Crisis?*, Cambridge: Cambridge University Press 1991, 18.
7. On the wider front, see T.F. Best, 'The Sociological Study of the New Testament: Promise and Peril of a New Discipline', *Scottish Journal of Theology*, 36 (1983), 181–194; also, S.K. Stowers, 'The Social Sciences and the Study of Early Christianity', in W.S. Green (ed.), *Approaches to Ancient Judaism*, Vol. V, Chico: Scholars Press 1985, 149–181.
8. R. Scroggs, 'The Earliest Christian Communities as Sectarian Movement', in J. Neusner, ed., *Christianity, Judaism and Other Greco-Roman Cults*, Part Two, Leiden: Brill 1975, 1–23.
9. Scroggs, 'Communities', 2–3.
10. Ibid., 3–7.
11. Ibid., 8, n. 26.

12. Ibid., 19–21.
13. Ibid., 21.
14. Ibid., 22.
15. Ibid., 1.
16. Ibid., 3.
17. On which see, for example, A.J. Malherbe, *Social Aspects of Early Christianity*, Philadelphia: Fortress Press 1983², 29–59.
18. See E.A. Judge, 'The Early Christians as a Scholastic Community', *Journal of Religious History*, 1 (1960–61), 4–15, 125–137.
19. W.A. Meeks, 'The Man from Heaven in Johannine Sectarianism', *Journal of Biblical Literature*, 91 (1972), 44–72. My references are to the reprinted version in J. Ashton, (ed.), *The Interpretation of John*, London: SPCK and Philadelphia: Fortress Press 1986, 141–173.
20. Meeks, 'Sectarianism', 162–163 (author's emphasis).
21. J. Louis Martyn, *History and Theology in the Fourth Gospel*, Nashville: Abingdon, 1968, 1979²; R.E. Brown, *The Community of the Beloved Disciple*, New York: Paulist Press and London: Chapman 1979; F.F. Segovia, *Love Relationships in the Johannine Tradition*, Chico: Scholars Press 1982; D. Rensberger, *Johannine Faith and Liberating Community*, Philadelphia: Westminster Press 1988 (= *Overcoming the World: Politics and Community in the Gospel of John*, London: SPCK 1989).
22. D.M. Smith, 'Johannine Christianity: Some Reflections on its Character and Delineation', *New Testament Studies*, 21 (1975), 224–248, at 223–224.
23. Meeks, 'Sectarianism', 144–145 (author's emphasis).
24. Since writing this, I notice that Mark Stibbe also finds Meeks' approach a persuasive and important advance in Johannine interpretation, in *John as Storyteller: Narrative Criticism and the Fourth Gospel*, Cambridge: Cambridge University Press 1992, esp. 61–63.
25. Meeks, 'Sectarianism', 147–152.
26. Brown, *Community*, 72, n. 128.
27. Meeks, 'Sectarianism', 163.
28. M. Hengel, *The Johannine Question*, London: SCM Press and Philadelphia: Trinity Press International 1990.
29. Meeks, 'Sectarianism', 145.
30. Hengel, *Johannine Question*, 104–105.
31. For an important critique of Meeks' functionalist sociology, see Stowers, 'Social Sciences', passim.
32. C.K. Barrett, 'St John: Social Historian', *Proceedings of the Irish Biblical Association*, 10 (1986), 26–39, at 26.
33. C.K. Barrett, 'School, Conventicle, and Church in the New Testament', in K. Aland and S. Meurer (eds), *Wissenschaft und Kirche. Festschrift für E. Lohse*, Bielefeld: Luther-Verlag 1989, 96–110.

34. One thinks, for example of Hengel's monograph, *Nachfolge und Charisma*, Berlin: Publisher 1968, translated into English by J.C. G. Greig as, *The Charismatic Leader and His Followers*, Edinburgh: T. & T. Clark 1981.
35. For a recent authoritative account, see Stephen Moore, *Literary Criticism and the Gospels: The Theoretical Challenge*, New Haven: Yale University Press 1989.
36. Brevard S. Childs, *The New Testament as Canon: An Introduction*, London: SCM Press and Philadelphia: Fortress Press 1984, 133.
37. P.F. Esler, *Community and Gospel in Luke-Acts*, Cambridge: Cambridge University Press 1987.
38. Esler, *Community*, 1.
39. See esp. Esler, *Community*, ch. 3.
40. Ibid., 67.
41. Ibid., 199.
42. See L.T. Johnson, *The Literary Function of Possessions in Luke-Acts*, Missoula: Scholars Press 1977, and compare Esler, *Community*, ch. 7.
43. L.T. Johnson, 'On Finding the Lukan Community: A Cautious Cautionary Tale', in P.J. Achtemeier (ed.), SBL 1979 *Seminar Papers Volume 1*, Missoula: Scholars Press 1979, 87–100.
44. Johnson, 'Tale', 89 (author's emphasis).
45. Johnson, 'Tale', 90.
46. Johnson, 'Tale', 92 (author's emphasis).
47. See J.H. Neyrey ed., *The Social World of Luke-Acts: Models for Interpretation*, Peabody, Mass: Hendrickson 1991.
48. Cf. Acts 5.17; 15.5; 26.5 for uses in relation to Judaism, and Acts 24.5, 14; 28.22 for its application by outsiders to Christianity. According to Barrett, 'School', 104, 'It is clear from these passages that Luke is familiar with the application of *hairesis* to the Jewish groups of Pharisees, Sadducees, and Essenes, and that he does not himself choose to apply it to Christianity, though he knows that others did so.'
49. Note Acts 9.2; 19.9, 23, 22.4; 24.14, 22; and cf. 2.28; 13.10; 16.17; 18.25, 26 – cited in Barrett, 'School', 103.
50. J.A. Overman, *Matthew's Gospel and Formative Judaism: The Social World of the Matthean Community*, Minneapolis: Fortress Press 1990. Diverse perspectives on Matthew as sectarian are taken in the essays by Gundry and White in the important volume edited by D.L. Balch, *Social History of the Matthean Community: Cross-Disciplinary Approaches*, Minneapolis: Fortress Press 1991. Cf also Graham Stanton's essay on 'Matthew's Gospel and the Damascus Document', in his *A Gospel for a New People*, Edinburgh: T. & T. Clark 1992, arguing that both texts are written for sectarian communities in sharp conflict with parent bodies from which they have separated recently.

51. H.C. Kee, *Community of the New Age*, London: SCM Press and Philadelphia: Westminster Press 1977.
52. W.A. Meeks, ' "Since then you would need to go out of the world": Group Boundaries in Pauline Christianity', in T.J. Ryan (ed.), *Critical History and Biblical Faith: New Testament Perspectives*, Billanova, Pa., Publisher 1979, 1–23.
53. W.A. Meeks, *The First Urban Christians: The Social World of the Apostle Paul*, New Haven and London: Yale University Press 1983.
54. Cf. also Meeks' book, *The Moral World of the First Christians*, Philadelphia: Westminster Press 1986; London: SPCK 1987, 98–108.
55. F. Watson, *Paul, Judaism and the Gentiles: A Sociological Approach*, Cambridge: Cambridge University Press 1986.
56. M.Y. MacDonald, *The Pauline Churches: A Socio-historical Study of Institutionalization in the Pauline and Deutero-Pauline Writings*, Cambridge: Cambridge University Press 1988.
57. J.H. Elliott, *A Home for the Homeless: A Sociological Exegesis of I Peter*, Philadelphia: Fortress Press and London: SCM Press 1981.
58. For a different analysis of I Peter, which was published in the same year as Elliott's book, but which interprets the Petrine household code as intended to promote greater *integration* into Graeco-Roman society, see D.L. Balch, *Let Wives Be Submissive: The Domestic Code in I Peter*, Chico: Scholars Press 1981.
59. I have explored this aspect further in *Discipleship and Family Ties According to Mark and Matthew*, PhD Thesis, King's College, University of London 1991.
60. So, too, Holmberg, *Sociology*, 112–113.
61. White, 'Boundaries', 14.
62. See further, S. Hauerwas and S. Long, 'Interpreting the Bible as a Political Act', *Religion and Intellectual Life*, VI (1989), 134–142. Note also the perceptive comment of White, 'Boundaries', 9: 'All too often the picture has been based on simplistic, idealized, or theologically tendentious reading of the New Testament documents, as in traditional Marxist historiography of early Christianity. It is no less in evidence elsewhere, as in the characteristic equation in Protestant historiography: first-century Judaism is seen by analogy with the medieval Catholic church, against which Jesus and the Reformers were parallel sectarian responses.'

8

A Future for the Commentary?*

Richard Coggins

Introduction

The ambiguous position of the teacher of biblical studies in a university is well known. She or he is likely to be regarded by academic colleagues as having another allegiance: to a church or religious group, an allegiance which must hamper that proper objectivity and detachment which traditionally have been demanded by academic study. But the academic study of the Bible is often regarded with the gravest suspicion in church circles, as tending to weaken the basis of faith by raising awkward questions about the Bible and its reliability.

If an ambiguity of this kind is characteristic of much academic study of the Bible, problems arise in particularly acute form in respect of the commentary. It has become axiomatic in serious biblical study that the proper companion to the detailed study of a biblical text is a commentary. Such a volume may concern itself with ensuring that the details of the original Hebrew or Greek text have been accurately transmitted; it may supply historical or geographical background information to enable the Bible to be read in the appropriate context; it may offer theological or moral or devotional reflections arising from the text to be studied. For the last century at least a whole variety of commentary series has striven to carry out

---

* The paper which follows was written for oral delivery at the conference on 'New Directions for Biblical Studies', and no attempt has been made to hide that origin. This must excuse the lack of scholarly footnotes and the over-frequent use of the first-person singular pronoun.

this purpose. But it is clear that commentaries are particularly susceptible to the kind of questioning which is raised by all biblical study: are they to be as objective and detached as possible or are they to strive to support the faith of the believer? What is to happen to the commentary as a literary form in the wake of a whole variety of new approaches to biblical study? It is with questions of this kind, as they affect future prospects for commentaries, that this paper is concerned.

1. *The revival of a genre*

Before we consider the likely future of the commentary as a genre it is worthwhile to recall its recent past, not least as a warning against too confident prediction. I remember that great excitement was caused in the Society for Old Testament Study some thirty years ago by the announcement that SCM Press in this country and Westminster Press in the USA were to publish a new series, 'The Old Testament Library'. Some of the books were to be general studies (Bright's *History of Israel* was I think the very first), but it would also include commentaries – von Rad on Genesis and Noth on Exodus, and also some new commentaries to be written for the series: James Barr on Genesis 1–11 appears on the early dust-jackets.

Barr's work regrettably never did appear, but that is a detail. The particular interest was caused by the fact that there were to be commentaries. For the species appeared to be defunct, as far as original writing in English was concerned – and there no doubt it was symptomatic that the two commentaries in the new series were to be translations of works written in German by Noth and von Rad. In theory the International Critical Commentary was still producing, but in practice no series of any consequence was then current in the English language, and our isolation from German scholarship (where the genre was still flourishing) was, I suspect, even greater then than it is today. At about the same time the announcement came through that the project which developed as the Anchor Bible was under way in the USA; by the mid-1960s the New Century Bible had started, together with the Cambridge Bible Commentary on the New English Bible at a more popular level, and these all concentrated on original work in English. It soon became difficult to imagine that there had ever been a drought, so copious was the flow. And of course I can only speak for the Old Testament side; I am not sure how far the New Testament had a similar period of abstinence. But it remains the case that for an extended period it appeared as if the commentary was almost extinct – just a few isolated volumes (C.R. North on Isaiah 40–55, for example) were the only exceptions. By contrast today, a quick look at my bookshelves revealed as many as eight English-language series currently in full spate, and I know of others which do not normally come my way. So at one level it seems absurd even to raise doubts about the future of the genre. Indeed, I have written to the editors of several series and all of them replied with enthusiasm as to the good health of the form in general and their own venture in particular. While I would not have expected them to announce that they had no hope for the future of their enterprise, their confidence was quite impressive. So while it would be folly to pretend that there are no uncertainties, and I shall devote most of my attention to them, it would also be unwise to ignore this very optimistic scenario.

Apart from any other consideration, I think this point is worth making at the outset because it is a reminder that fashions change in this, as in other fields of human endeavour.

2. Translation and commentary

Some of what must be said as we look to the future must be little more than truism, but I hope that that may be allowed as part of the larger picture. Thus, I do not for a moment suppose that it is possible to allow the Bible, or any other ancient text, to 'speak for itself', to be its own interpreter. Many students embarking on Hebrew or Greek for the first time give the impression of harbouring the delusion that the authors of the biblical text actually knew English, so that there is somewhere there a 'real' meaning of the words and phrases they are struggling with; but even when we widen our horizons somewhat there are plenty of problems remaining. The New English Bible Old Testament was described on its first appearance as 'a *midrash* on the Hebrew Bible'; it is notorious that the very process of translation from one language into another involves the kind of choice which is in itself effectively a commentary; and there is therefore in every version an element of commentary. It is a topic which has been widely explored in recent years, and I shall simply assume its underlying importance here.

3. *The inevitability of ideology*

Almost every feature of every commentary will be value-laden. There will no doubt be some factual information which must be conveyed for the ignorant or innocent reader to be able to make sense of what she or he reads, but rare indeed will be the cases where that information is, or can be, conveyed free of ideological overtones. Thus, if I may use the experience of editing a *Dictionary of Biblical Interpretation* as an illustration, it soon became clear that an article on 'Theological Geography' was essential; from the beginning of the Bible to the end, from the 'garden in Eden, in the east' to the 'holy city, new Jerusalem, coming down out of heaven', an overwhelming number of what might be taken to be innocent geographical references need more than a simple street plan to put the reader on the right track. How other than by a commentary can the appropriate warnings be sounded?

But it is not long before difficulties emerge; how much of our Bible's geography is 'theological'? If one is reading the Book of Exodus, does one need to know the geography of the appropriate area, possible stretches of water which might at times dry up, and the like? Or is all that information essentially irrelevant, the result of asking the wrong questions of the text? Here the aspect of being value-laden emerges: some form of guidance is needed.

Issues of that kind will produce very different answers from different types of commentary, which at once suggests that there are complexities within the genre, and I want next to reflect on some of them.

4. *Commentary as objective?*

My first difficulty arises from the actual word 'commentary'. It is most often used, I suppose, in relation to sporting events. On television or radio we are used to 'commentators' who tell us what is going on and interpret its significance, who according to their skill and our receptivity either provide helpful guidance or get in the way of the real action. For me one of the most irritating things about sports commentators is when they become too obviously partisan, praising the efforts of the gallant Britons who are far back in the field rather than giving an assessment of the skill of the winner. Total impartiality may be impossible; but at least a fair account of the proceedings is called for.

But where does the biblical commentator stand on these criteria? Here is the job-description as laid down by a selection of current commentary series. All my quotations are taken from descriptive leaflets or dust-jackets. The *Word Biblical Commentary* proclaims itself 'the best in evangelical critical scholarship'. I'm not clear whether a test is applied before commissions are put out, but clearly 'evangelical' here must at least mean acceptance of the authority of the text to be commented upon. So too with the *Tyndale* series, where authors are allowed to 'represent the stated views of sincere fellow Christians'. Again I am not clear how sincerity is tested or how 'Christians' are defined, but there seems to be no place for the views of non-Christians. In some ways more alarming still, the *International Theological Commentary* announces the necessity of transcending 'the parochialism of Western civilization', and asserts that its contributors are Christians who affirm the witness of the New Testament. By comparison the assertion of the *New Century Bible*, claiming no more than that it will reflect 'the contemporary relevance of the biblical text', seems modest indeed.

When set against all this even the most little-Englander among sports commentators seems balanced and impartial. This immediately raises another question concerning the nature of the commentary.

5. Who is the commentary for?

Is biblical commentary to be understood simply in the way that those job-descriptions seemed to imply, as an exercise carried on within the confines of the community of believers? Such an exercise may indeed be entirely legitimate, but it raises questions whether 'commentary' is now quite the appropriate word. How often in examinations when questions have asked for 'Comment upon the following passages' have answers been marked down when they resembled sermons, uncritically and unquestioningly accepting and relaying the thrust of the biblical passage? Should commentators be similarly penalized, or is that part of their brief?

Let me put this another way. We are all familiar with, or at least aware of, the genre of devotional commentaries. Down the centuries this could be said to have been the essential basis of commentaries;

Cassiodorus on the Psalms from the sixth century, recently translated in a new edition, comes into this category; so, too, does Calvin
from the sixteenth, though his devotions will be a little stringent for
some. Are we now to assume that there is a complete divorce
between the academic and the devotional in the commentary?
Curiously, the point that first struck me when I was asked to review a
volume in a new series of devotional commentaries entitled 'Message
of Biblical Spirituality' was how similar much of it seemed to be to
any other kind of commentary.

As I have mentioned already, one of the pieces of homework that I
engaged in as preparation for this paper was to write to the editors of
several well-known series and to find out from them their views on
the topic I am addressing. I received some very interesting answers,
and shall refer to them more than once as I go on. On this topic let me
quote Professor Donald Wiseman, general editor of the Tyndale
Series, to which I have already referred. His view is that the series sets
out to provide the insights of academic research on matters relating
to the Bible, to link with particular translations, and hopes both to
'fill this niche and to include "devotional" aspects ... which may be
increasingly sought for'. He is optimistic that the commentary, thus
understood, has a continuing role, though he is concerned about the
undue proliferation of new series.

An obvious response to such a viewpoint would be to suggest that
it may be true for the Roman Catholics of the new series to which I
referred, or for the conservative evangelicals who will read the
Tyndale series – both groups are writing for a captive audience, those
who are already committed to Christian belief. Let me therefore set
alongside Professor Wiseman one whose views would not normally
be bracketted with his. Professor Dennis Nineham, once regarded as
an *enfant terrible* of New Testament studies, apparently found no
problem in the introduction to his commentary on St Mark's Gospel
in referring to Jesus as 'Our Lord'. Is he as commentator the
churchman, writing for fellow-believers, or the impartial scholar?

The underlying point remains: must a commentary always 'support' the biblical view? Do we always have to identify ourselves with
the biblical characters whose words and actions were endorsed by
the final editors of the material? It is certainly an interesting issue
how far the accepted ideologies which dominate both Hebrew Bible
and New Testament have come to shape our agenda.

The views of Brevard Childs are, of course, relevant here. If *the* way to approach the material is as 'scripture', if the decisions of the later canonical communities are to be determinative, then it is surely logical that not only their decisions about which books were to be received as scripture, but also the attitudes and world-views embodied in those books, should be regarded as normative. On this understanding neutrality is not to be aimed at, is probably not even possible; legitimately to comment on biblical texts is to accept the world which they offer to us. Let me offer one more illustration in this field. There can scarcely be a biblical book where historical-critical discussion has failed to raise questions concerning genuineness: is this prophetic oracle original or a later addition? Did Paul write this epistle or is it by a later Paulinist? And so on. Now it seems to me that far too often the discussion of these issues is shaped by a hidden agenda, which is very closely related to what are taken to be the requirements of the faith-community. Most commonly those demands exert pressure in the direction of finding things to be original and genuine, and so it comes as something of a surprise if, for example in the *Tyndale* series we find a passage taken as secondary or a book attributed to an author other than the reputed one. But this pressure can also work the other way round, and has often done so particularly in the German tradition. If scripture is to be the basis of the community's faith, then rigorous historical investigation must be engaged in so as to establish as securely as possible the real origin of that scripture, and if this involves a radical scepticism, so be it. If I am about to make a journey through a minefield, I should welcome radical scepticism on the part of my guide: 'I expect it's all right' will not give me much confidence. In each case, though in different ways, the desire for impartial investigation of the truth can be overruled by ideological considerations.

6. *The historical-critical model abandoned?*

So far, I have concerned myself with the commentator's stance, and the question whether objectivity, neutrality, is desirable or even achievable; and then with what kind of readership we are to envisage. But there are of course other problems which have been raised concerning the place of the commentary, and it is to some of them that I want to turn briefly now.

A great feature of the historical-critical method at its best has been its claim to accuracy, objectivity, exactness of detail – a careful assessment of all the relevant evidence both internal and external which could help the reader to understand the circumstances of composition of an ancient book, its historical reliability and so on. It was interesting to hear from Professor Christopher Evans in a recent conversation how he felt that these qualities, demonstrated to the best of his ability in his large-scale commentary on St Luke's Gospel were coming to be regarded as old-fashioned. 'Reader-response', he said, 'is all the rage nowadays.'

I think he overstated the position, but there is clearly something in it, and this brings us back to the difficulties alluded to by Leslie Houlden in his article in the *Dictionary of Biblical Interpretation* on 'New Testament Commentaries'. It is interesting that he in effect reinforces Christopher Evans' dismay when he suggests that the 'theologically more significant' approach in the future may be along the lines sketched out by Ricoeur, which will imply 'an approach which abandons the uncommitted neutrality of the historian and reintroduces faith into the process of apprehending the text'. My doubt here is one that I have already expressed; I am sceptical as to whether faith, in that sense, has ever left this process.

7. *Reader-response at work*

Let me leave that point for the moment and turn to the related and very obvious difficulty confronting the commentary: the increased variety of approaches to the biblical texts now being promoted. One of the best commentaries that I have read in recent years is that of David Clines on the Book of Job. It takes him 500 pages to complete chapters 1–20 of the biblical text, so it is a considerable achievement to have sustained a comprehensible flow of argument over such length. It is instructive to notice what he has done in one part of his introduction; he has offered a section entitled 'Readings', in which he sketches a feminist, a vegetarian, a materialist, and a Christian reading of the biblical book. I use the word 'sketches' deliberately, for surely David Clines would readily acknowledge that these are no more than that, brief outlines (roughly two pages each) of what the book of Job might have to offer to those who approach it from such viewpoints. But he stresses, surely rightly, that 'in no activity of life, and certainly not in reading the Bible, can one hide or abandon one's values without doing violence to one's own integrity'. Here is the positive affirmation of the 'reader-response' about which

Christopher Evans was so doubtful. Since the four readings Clines has offered are only a selection of the world-views which might form one's starting-point, and since all of them could be set out at much greater length than he has offered there, the potential for variety and sheer size is alarming indeed.

This is a point recognized in a most interesting letter I received, in response to my request, from David Hubbard, President of Fuller Seminary, and General Editor of the *Word* Series. He wonders whether David Clines' approach is likely to set a new trend, and, if so, 'what limits or guidelines are needed? Would it be better to encourage all commentators to display at some length in the introduction their hermeneutical presuppositions and to refer to them in salient passages throughout the commentary?'. He went on in his letter to tell me that one contributor to his series had made some negative comments on other commentaries for the lack of this concern; and that – regretfully – these comments had been edited out of the published version.

8. Whose model?

Relevant at this point seems to be an issue raised by one of my fellow-contributors: Mark Brett in his *Biblical Criticism in Crisis?*, published in 1991. In that book Brett was discussing the future of the canonical approach as exemplified by the work of Brevard Childs in particular; and toward the end of the book he draws attention to two distinct models of the church: a 'top-down' model, in which the church is 'guided by benevolent authorities' (p. 165), where the expertise in biblical matters is confined to a small elite, who not only provide the answers to the simple faithful but also make certain that only the proper questions are asked. Thus (these are my own examples, not Mark Brett's) one is not allowed to suggest that Abraham was crazy when he thought he heard a divine voice telling him to go and kill his son; or that Paul would have been better off if he had stuck with his Pharisee upbringing; or whatever.

But that model of the church would now be widely challenged: 'a more egalitarian ecclesiology would want to prevent the interpretation of scripture from becoming the preserve of learned and powerful elites' (p. 165). The role of feminist scholars in challenging this role is well-known; as I was preparing this material I was reading a book by a German feminist scholar, Hildegunde Wöller, who regarded the

underlying story of a good part of the Hebrew Bible as the seizure by
men, in the interests of a patriarchal structure of society, of roles
previously open to women. The challenges from liberation and other
perspectives have also raised questions about more traditional readings. Brett goes on in a most entertaining way to note the role of
universities in all this: 'university experts have vested interests in
making biblical study difficult, and thus worthy of a place in the
university' (p. 166).

9. A role for the history of interpretation?

One more area of reflection and then I will try to bring these rather
disparate thoughts together. Virtually everything that I have said so
far has related either to the very beginning of the process of trans-
mission of the material, or to the very end of the process in our own
day. Commentaries are characteristically *either* trying to get back to
the original: re-creating the eighth century BCE or the first century CE,
placing our characters in their setting, explaining what their words
would have meant to their contemporary situation; *or* they are
seeking to establish the relevance of biblical material to the present-
day audience, however 'relevance' and 'the present-day audience'
may be defined.

But to do that is to ignore the enormous weight and wealth of
biblical interpretation which has taken place down the centuries. If I
may be allowed one more reference to the *Dictionary of Biblical
Interpretation*, to me as editor some of the most absorbing contributions came from those who wrote on the Bible in art or in music,
opening up to me worlds of whose existence I was vaguely aware but
which really existed in a separate part of my mind from 'proper'
biblical study.

Where then in a commentary on Isaiah is the place of the ox and
the ass in 1.3, a theme not taken up by the New Testament birth-
narratives, but seized upon by patristic and mediaeval commentators
and popularized by the Christmas crib in innumerable modern
churches? Is all that simply a false understanding that we have grown
out of? Should it not be put to creative use by a modern commentator? Texts have an after-life, and on any showing this is an
important part of the after-life of the book of Isaiah; what is to be
done about it? Again, any respectable commentary on Genesis 1 will
have reference to *Enuma Elish* and other ancient Near Eastern

creation stories; is there any place there for a reference to Haydn's *Creation* and the perception of God's creative power that that embodies?

10. Conclusions

In the end, therefore, it seems to me that there are two basic problems which must shape our perception of the future of the commentary.

(*a*) There is the increasing complexity of the task. Here Christopher Evans' point is relevant; if reader response criticisms are to set the agenda then there is a sense in which anything goes (or anything goes in) because of the sheer variety of readers. David Clines' feminists, vegetarians and materialists are but a mere sample.

Now in one sense of course this is real gain. At the moment my experience must be that of many people; I am working through a biblical text and I come to a problem. I turn for help to the commentaries; and discover that they all say the same thing. Sometimes that appears to be almost literally the case, and the amount of unacknowledged borrowing that goes on might in some uncharitable circles be construed as the problem for the commentary. But that is not really the point; it is notoriously difficult to know where 'gratitude for the insights offered by ...' turns into plagiarism. The real point, however, is the predictability of so many commentaries, and the absence of what might be called lateral thinking, of the kind implied above by the references to the ox and ass in Isaiah or Haydn in Genesis. So, some increase in variety must surely be great gain; but how much the genre and the market that supports it will stand may pose real problems.

(*b*) The other problem is the nature of 'the guilds which are keepers of the texts'. Many will recognize the phrase as a characteristic expression of Robert Carroll, and he will be quoted more fully below. Now clearly if we picture our texts as Bible, Holy Book, then those who belong to particular communities which esteem those texts in that sense will feel that theirs is the right and duty of providing the appropriate commentary. But immediately any kind of outward movement takes place trouble is looming for that approach.

Various churches have proclaimed the 1990s as a 'decade of evangelism'. It is not entirely clear to me what that means, but at the very least it must presumably mean that the claims of those churches are open to scrutiny by those who may be the recipients of such evangelism. And among those claims will be that of special status for the Bible. And if that claim is made, will it stand up under such scrutiny? Now to enter into that question in any seriousness would require at least another paper, but let me end with a point that arises from that whole issue: Can the commentary be kept distinct from the propaganda weapon?

I quote Robert Carroll again, this time from the paper which he read to the December 1991 meeting of the Society for Old Testament Study, of which he has kindly let me have a copy. He in turn quotes Andersen and Freedman's massive Anchor Bible on Hosea, noting from the discussion of chapters 1–3 their assertion that 'the perversion of sex and an excessive preoccupation with it are common factors in Canaanite religion' (p. 158). It is not difficult to see how one-sided (to put it no more strongly) this is: and Carroll predictably has some fun with this: 'What are their sources for this evaluation of Canaanite religion? Would a sociological analysis of Canaanite texts and material remains establish both the perversion of sex and an excessive preoccupation with it? And who will define or quantify "excessive" or "perversion"? What is going on here in this commentary?' He goes on to note that what at least can be gleaned from the text is the apparent distrust of some biblical writers for foreigners and women.

There is more; some of it good knockabout stuff, but underlying it all is a very serious point. Let me illustrate it by another example. If one asks a reasonably well-educated non-churchperson what she/he knows about the Pharisees, the answer is likely to be some version of the Gospel material in its more unflattering expression. How far does a commentator on the Gospels regard it as her/his primary duty to say that Jesus was wrong in his estimate of the Pharisees? The tension may be eased by saying that Matthew 23 is a later elaboration by the evangelist: is that decision reached on purely objective grounds or is it motivated by the feeling that Jesus cannot have been so grossly unfair? I only ask; you will see the sort of dilemma that arises between the commentator pictured as one who is in effect an additional minister, supporting the expectations of the faithful community (thus many commentators down the ages) and the commentator as objective seeker after the truth however awkward that may be. We need to remember here what Noll said (*Journal of Biblical Literature* 1987; and again I owe this quotation to Robert Carroll) that 'all Bible scholarship is dogmatic and all Bible scholarship is political' (perhaps 'ideological' would express the point more clearly).

I should end by admitting that I have recently agreed to write a commentary myself for one of the series to which I have alluded. The reader must not be cynical, trying to see how many of these problems I manage to cope with, but be sympathetic to the increasingly difficult task of the commentary writer in this climate which has led to greater self-scrutiny than for a very long time.

Contributors

STEPHEN BARTON taught first at Salisbury and Wells Theological College and is now lecturer in New Testament at the University of Durham. He is author of *Spirituality and the Gospels*.

MARK BRETT was for a time lecturer in Old Testament at Lincoln Theological College and has now returned to his native Australia where he teaches at Whitley College, Melbourne. He is author of *Biblical Criticism in Crisis?*.

RICHARD COGGINS teaches Old Testament at King's College, London. He has written a number of books, most recently *Introducing the Old Testament*, and is joint editor of *A Dictionary of Biblical Interpretation*.

WERNER JEANROND teaches systematic theology at Trinity College, Dublin, and has a special interest in hermeneutics. His books include *Text and Interpretation* and most recently, *Theological Hermeneutics*.

STEPHEN MOORE, who was formerly at Trinity College, Dublin is now assistant Professor of Religion at Wichita State University. He is the author of *Literary Criticism and the Gospels* and *Mark and Luke in Poststructuralist Perspectives: Jesus Begins to Write*.

PHYLLIS TRIBLE, who is a leading feminist Old Testament/ Hebrew Bible scholar, teaches Old Testament at Union Theological Seminary. Her writings include *God and the Rhetoric of Sexuality* and *Texts of Terror: Literary-Feminist Readings of Biblical Narratives*.

FRANCIS WATSON is lecturer in New Testament studies at King's College, London. He is author of *Paul, Judaism and the Gentiles*, and of *Text, Church and World: Towards a Theological Hermeneutic for Biblical Studies* (forthcoming).

FRANCES YOUNG is Edward Cadbury Professor of Theology in the University of Birmingham. She has written many books, most recently *The Art of Performance: Towards a Theology of Holy Scripture*.